AFTER BERNADETTE

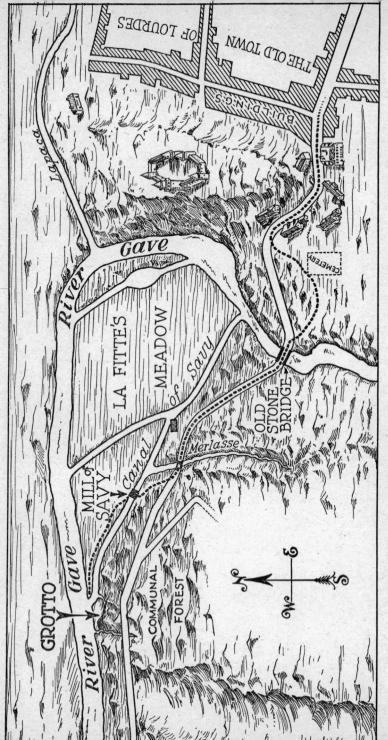

Lourdes and the land about the grotto as it was in Bernadette's day. The broken line shows approximately the path she took to the grotto

After Bernadette

THE STORY of MODERN LOURDES

DON SHARKEY

THE BRUCE PUBLISHING COMPANY
MILWAUKEE

Nihil obstat: H. B. RIES
Imprimatur: ✠ MOSES E. KILEY, Archbishop of Milwaukee
May 28, 1945

◆◆◆◆◆◆

To Our Lady of Lourdes

◆◆◆◆◆◆

CONTENTS

PART I

INTRODUCTION

PART II

BERNADETTE AND THE APPARITIONS

PART III

THE SHRINE'S FIRST YEARS

PART IV

OUR LADY VERSUS "SCIENCE"

8

Contents

PART V

MODERN LOURDES

PART VI

THE CURED AND THE UNCURED

APPENDIX

PART I

INTRODUCTION

CHAPTER I

TWO NOVELISTS WENT TO LOURDES

TWO novelists went to Lourdes. One was Émile Zola; the other was Franz Werfel. Both had achieved no small amount of fame as writers. Neither was a Christian. Each wrote a novel which was based upon his visit.

The novels were in direct contradiction to each other. The one author was firmly convinced that the events which take place at Lourdes are miraculous. The other reported that they are due entirely to natural causes, that the claims of miracles are so much humbug.

The facts were there for both to examine. Why such conflicting reports?

Which of the novelists was right? Which was wrong?

Let us examine the facts in each case.

Many remarkable events have taken place at Lourdes in the past ninety years, and the story of Franz Werfel and *The Song of Bernadette* is not the least remarkable of them.

Franz Werfel, a Bohemian Jew, served as a sergeant in the Austrian army during World War I. He was one of the earliest opponents of Nazism. In 1922, eleven years before the Nazis came to power in Germany, he wrote a play entitled *Schweiger*. This play, he tells us, "depicted the Nazi type in the naked frightfulness of its consistency." It appeared in Berlin and a number of other German cities. The Nazis, who never forgave an enemy, marked Werfel for punishment. He was sure that this punishment would be death.

After Hitler's rise to power, Werfel dared not set foot in Germany. Later Austria fell to the Nazis, and that country also was closed to him. Next Czechoslovakia fell, and his own native city of Prague was in the hands of the enemy. He was a man without a country.

Werfel fled to France and was living there in 1940 when that country was locked in mortal combat with Nazi Germany. Suddenly everything was chaos. The French army, which had been rated the finest in the world, collapsed. With no organized resistance to stop them, the Nazis were free to overrun all France.

All those who had any reason to fear personal reprisals from the Nazis — and there were thousands of such unhappy souls — fled toward the Spanish border. A few succeeded in getting across into Spain, but the escape of most of them was cut off when the Germans seized the frontier town of Hendaye. Werfel and his wife were among those who found themselves in the French Pyrenees with all means of escape cut off. He describes the situation thus: "Crowded together in the southwest corner of France, the confused throng of fugitive peoples, Poles, Czechs, Dutch, Belgians, French — soldiers and civilians, men, women, and children — moved about in aimless circles without food and shelter in heavily laden, sometimes bullet-ridden cars. The frontiers were relentlessly closed; the consuls pitilessly bureaucratic! And in all the crowds lurked the spying forces of the Gestapo, calmly spotting their victims."

The district around Lourdes was an island of charity in the tumultuous, pitiless sea. The church and even the government officials did everything they could to help the refugees. They provided them with rooms in the hotels, food, clothing, even a little money. They steadfastly refused to turn the fugitives over to the Germans, an act of incredible courage. No wonder the refugees flocked to Lourdes. There were 80,000 of them there at one time.

Among these thousands was Franz Werfel. Thus he became acquainted with the history of Lourdes of which he says he "had hitherto had but the most superficial knowledge."

Those were terrifying days. The Nazi machine was relentless. The armistice, which was signed while Werfel was in Lourdes, provided that France turn over certain civilians to the Nazis. Werfel was sure that he was one of the civilians. His plight seemed desperate. "Had my day come? Those in the know claimed to have seen my name on the extradition lists. Was there a power on earth to help me?"

Although this was a time of terrible dread and uncertainty, it was also a time of great spiritual consolation. Carla Zawish, M.D., a refugee from Austria, was in Lourdes at that time. She tells us: "The ecclesiastical authorities did their best to open the channels of grace for all those souls in distress. A retreat was preached for the refugees, with catechetical conferences; the Church of the Rosary overflowed with hearers, and loud-speakers carried the preachers' words over the entire esplanade. Conversions were frequent; indifferent persons found themselves again at the Communion table. Never was the grotto deserted from morning till night; even in winter when ice lay on the esplanade or torrential rains inundated it, in spite of nobody having good shoes in those days. There were, of course, the incorrigibly indifferent and the skeptical; but at least they refrained from scoffing, subdued as it were by the mystery."

Werfel was greatly affected by Lourdes. Dr. Zawish says of him, "I saw the deep emotion of Franz Werfel, the future author of *The Song of Bernadette;* I had known him and his wife in Vienna, how long ago? and now we met again just here. Never before had he been so profoundly shaken in all his being. A new world had opened before him, and he plunged into it with all his eagerness. I liked to answer his questions because I saw what was going on was much more than merely the enthusiasm of a poet."

Even though the net of the Nazis was closing in on him, this was a time of great significance for Werfel. He listened to the story of Bernadette over and over again and was thrilled by it. He became acquainted with the wondrous healings that take place at Lourdes. He tells us, "One day in my great distress I made a vow. I vowed that if I escaped from this desperate situation and reached the saving shore of America, I would put off all other tasks and sing, as best I could, the song of Bernadette."

Werfel did escape, and he made good his promise. After thousands and thousands of persons had read the book, millions more became familiar with the story of Bernadette by seeing the movie based on it.

*   *   *

Émile Zola was a French novelist who enjoyed great popularity in certain circles toward the end of the nineteenth century. Zola denied the existence of the supernatural. To him, man was nothing but an animal. Nobility, spiritual greatness, self-sacrifice were of no account. He looked upon himself as a scientist who collected "human documents." Science, he said, left no room for the spiritual.

In 1892, Zola announced that he intended to visit Lourdes and investigate the cures reported to have taken place there. He would examine the facts very thoroughly and scientifically and then make his report; he would let the world know the truth about Lourdes. The announcement was widely hailed. Newspapers sent reporters to accompany him on his trip. The officials of Lourdes said they would be more than happy to co-operate with him in any way possible. Several Catholic publications said that the announcement was no doubt an indication that Zola had seen the error of his ways and would soon do an about face.

After a two weeks' visit to Lourdes, Zola returned and prepared his report in the form of a novel.

Two characters stand out in Zola's novel *Lourdes*. They are Elise Rouquet and La Grivotte. The former was described as having a horrible lupus which had gnawed away at her nose and mouth, "almost obliterating the traces of what once were pleasing womanly lineaments." La Grivotte was a consumptive whose lungs were almost eaten away by tuberculosis.

In the novel, Elise Rouquet bathed her face with Lourdes water for a whole morning and gradually the sore seemed to grow paler in color. Dr. Bonamy of the Medical Bureau advised Elise to continue using the water as a lotion and return each day for further examination. To the other doctors he said, "At all events, gentlemen, there are signs of improvement in this case — that is beyond doubt."

La Grivotte, according to Zola, came dancing into the office of the Medical Bureau shouting, "I am cured! I am cured!" She had not been bathed in the icy water of the baths for longer than three minutes before she felt her strength return to her body. But alas, the cure proved to be temporary. La Grivotte died on the train on her way home.

That was Zola's report on Lourdes. The one patient was cured slowly and imperfectly. The other seemed for a short time to be completely cured, but she died soon afterwards. Clearly her cure had been due to autosuggestion. Zola attributed all the cures of Lourdes to hynotism, the shock caused by the cold water, the "healing inspiration of the crowd," and the curative effect on disordered nerves of the monotonous roll of the Litanies and the *Aves*.

Zola's book was enthusiastically applauded by those who did not believe in the supernatural. Zola, they said, had gone to Lourdes with an open mind, ready to accept or reject miracles according to the evidence which he found. He came away convinced that all cures were due to purely natural causes. This book, they said, should end forever the superstition of Lourdes.

Werfel or Zola? Whom is one to believe? Werfel was in danger of his life and was perhaps overwrought emotionally. Zola looked at the situation coolly and dispassionately from a scientific point of view. Isn't there a good chance that Zola was right, Werfel wrong?

It is very easy to check Zola's story, for his characters were based on real persons. Elise Rouquet was in reality Marie Lemarchand, and her disease was just as terrible as Zola described it. La Grivotte was Marie Lebranchu. She was so racked with consumption that the doctors begged her not to make the trip to Lourdes. Both these women were on the train that brought Zola to Lourdes, and he studied their cases very carefully.

Marie Lemarchand, the Elise Rouquet of the novel, arrived at Lourdes on August 20. She was cured the next morning while bathing in the *piscine*. There was no continued washing as Zola had reported. Her cure was immediate and complete, not slow and imperfect. She lived for many more years, married, and eventually became the mother of five children. The old disease never returned.

Marie Lebranchu, Zola's La Grivotte, was cured just as completely as the novelist recorded, but there was a slight difference in the sequel. Zola had her die on the way home from Lourdes. In reality, she lived for many years and never had a return of the consumption of which she had been cured. When she finally died, it was of an entirely different cause.

The fact that La Grivotte continued to live, despite the fact that he had had her die, became embarrassing to Zola. In 1895 he went to see Marie Lebranchu. Later, in an interview, she told the story of Zola's visit.

"He told me that if I wanted to leave Paris and go to Belgium with my husband, he would see to it that we should not want for anything."

"Then he suggested that you go to Brussels?"

"No, not to Brussels nor to any other large city. We would have to live in a country place which he would get for us himself. Then he pulled out his pocketbook and took a bundle of notes from it. I do not know how much it was, for he did not count them. He held them out to me saying, 'Here, this will do for your first needs. It will be enough for a month. In that time, I will look for what you want and I will myself secure you a place.'"

"Did you accept the offer?"

"For a moment I was tempted to do so, for we were destitute. But my husband, making up his mind quite suddenly, went up to Mr. Zola, took him by the arm, and put him out. Mr. Zola left, and I never saw him again."

Dr. Boissarie was head of the Lourdes Medical Bureau at the time of Zola's visit. He appears in the novel as Dr. Bonamy. He was, naturally enough, indignant at Zola's "report" of the cures. Some years later, he met the novelist and demanded to know why he had made La Grivotte die when in reality she was quite well.

Zola replied, "I am the absolute master of my characters. I make them live or die to suit my pleasure. Madame Lebranchu, being healed, has no ground to complain. I don't believe in miracles, anyhow; *should I see all the sick in Lourdes get well in a moment, I still would not believe.*"

Zola is typical of a certain type of mind which is determined not to believe despite any evidence it may behold, no matter how convincing. Persons of his type have tried to discredit Lourdes ever since the Virgin first appeared to Bernadette. They closed the grotto while the apparitions were still taking place and tried to prevent the crowds from going there. Later, they wrote untrue articles in the newspapers to convince people that the whole thing was a fraud. At the beginning of this century, they tried to close Lourdes in the name of hygiene. All these attempts have ended in failure and have succeeded only in swelling the number of pilgrims flocking to Lourdes.

The conflict is not between Werfel and Zola, just as it was not between Bernadette and the Police Commissioner who tried to keep her from going to the grotto. It is a conflict between good and evil. It is a conflict between the Blessed Virgin and Satan.

After Satan, in the form of a serpent, caused Adam and Eve to be cast out of the Garden of Eden, God promised that the Woman would crush the serpent with her heel. The Woman appeared on earth after several thousand years and became the Mother of the Saviour. She is always trying to guide people into heaven; Satan is trying to lure them into the lowest depths of hell.

During the fourth appearance of the Blessed Virgin to Bernadette, the girl, according to J. B. Estrade who lived in Lourdes at the time, heard a great outburst of sinister voices which seemed to come from the bowels of the earth. The voices questioned, contradicted, interrupted each other, like the shouts of a quarrelsome crowd. One voice, louder than the others, cried, "Escape! Escape for your life." The Lady raised her head and frowned in the direction of the river. The voices seemed to be seized with fear, then to be scattering in all directions, and finally they died away.

When Satan himself was unable to prevent the processions at Lourdes — the processions for which the Blessed Virgin had asked — he tried working through human beings. This is not to say that Zola or any other individual was consciously obeying the devil's wishes. Zola did not believe in the supernatural at all; he did not, therefore, believe in Satan any more than he did in the Virgin. Nevertheless, Satan must have been pleased, indeed, when Zola made his report about Lourdes.

Zola sought to discredit Lourdes and succeeded only in discrediting himself. Angered by Zola's attack, a number of prominent persons, including the brilliant French novelist Huysmans, sprang to its defense. Lourdes was again given widespread attention. The number of pilgrims increased at once. The Virgin had defeated Satan.

World War II came and stopped the great pilgrimages to Lourdes. Satan had a few moments of triumph, but they were brief indeed. Lourdes was crowded with refugees, and a great number of conversions took place. Franz Werfel was driven there by the war, learned the story of Lourdes, and went forth to sing the song of Bernadette to all the world. Even though people in distant places could no longer visit Lourdes, they learned its story, and devotion to the Blessed Virgin increased immeasurably. If it had not been for the war, this particular Song of Bernadette would never have been sung. Once again the Woman had crushed the Serpent — as she will until the end of time.

The story of Bernadette has been told many times; the story of Lourdes has not been told so often. Many persons, for instance, who read Werfel's book or saw the movie must have wondered, "What has taken place at Lourdes since the time of Bernadette?" This book is an attempt to give an answer to that question.

In telling the story of Lourdes, Bernadette cannot be left out, for the story would not be complete without her. The principal emphasis, however, in this book is on Lourdes itself. In all the world, there is no other place like it. A million pilgrims go there every year to pay their homage to the Blessed Virgin; that is more people than took part in all the Crusades of the Middle Ages. Wonderful cures take place, cures which cannot be explained by natural means despite the efforts of Zola and others to do so. And more wonderful than the cures of bodies are the cures of souls.

It is a fascinating story and a consoling one, the story of this Miracle City in the High Pyrenees.

PART II

BERNADETTE AND THE APPARITIONS

CHAPTER II

THE SOUBIROUS FAMILY

LOUISE CASTEROT married François Soubirous on January 9, 1843, in the parish church of Lourdes. Louise was the second eldest daughter of a comfortably situated milling family, and François was a journeyman miller who was not very well off. The wedding did not attract a great deal of attention even in Lourdes, none at all outside the little mountain town. Who could have dreamed that from this union would come a daughter who was destined to be a great saint, instrumental in changing Lourdes from an obscure village to a world famous shrine?

The Casterots operated a mill at the extreme north limits of Lourdes, in the quarter known as Lapaca. Justin Casterot died in 1841, leaving a widow, four daughters, and a young son. The eldest daughter, Bernarde, was already married, and so the duty of operating the mill and supporting the family fell to Louise. When she married, her husband became the manager of the mill.

Under the new management, receipts soon decreased. François had a somewhat ungracious manner which did not attract customers, and his work was frequently careless. The flour which he sent out was not always in good condition and was not always delivered at the time promised. Louise was so young and so blinded by her affection for her husband that she did not notice his haphazard manner of doing business.

The Soubirous' first child, a girl, was born on January 7, 1844. The family was still in rather favorable circumstances at that time. She was baptized the next day by Abbé Forgues, then the curé of Lourdes. Her godfather was her twelve-year-old cousin, Jean-Marie Vedere. Her godmother was her Aunt Bernarde. She was given the name Marie-Bernard — after St. Bernard, the famous doctor of the church who was known for his great devotion to the Blessed Virgin. Custom soon changed this name to the diminutive Bernadette, the name by which she is known to the world today.

When Bernadette was only six months old, she was obliged to leave home. Her mother was expecting another child, and so she sent the little girl to the neighboring town of Bartes. There she lived with Marie Laguës who is sometimes called Bernadette's foster mother. Bernadette remained at Bartes for fifteen months, returning to Lourdes in October, 1845.

There, at the mill, she grew up, a round-faced, bright-eyed, ebony-haired child. She was fair and delicate, and when she was seven years old, she developed trouble with her breathing. This condition was called asthma during her lifetime, but there seems to be little doubt that what she had was tuberculosis. Her parents were glad when they could send her on occasional visits to her foster mother at Bartes because there she could breathe the pure mountain air.

Business at the mill continued to fall off. In 1845, the Soubirous were no longer able to pay the lease on the mill and were evicted. Both father and mother worked at any odd job they could find in an attempt to support themselves and their children. (Their children now numbered three. Five had been born, but two had died.) Time after time they were forced out on the street because they could not pay their rent.

The winter of 1855 was especially bad in the Pyrenees, and the Soubirous were never sure of having a roof over their heads. Aunt Bernarde, knowing that Bernadette was too delicate to stand such conditions, took the girl to live with her for seven or eight months. When the coldest part of the winter was over, Bernadette returned to her family.

By the fall of 1856, the Soubirous had become such notoriously bad tenants that no one would rent to them. It was then that they went to Andre Sajoux, a cousin of Louise, to ask him if they could live in the unused cell room of the abandoned city jail. This jail was known to the townspeople as *le cachot,* the dungeon. Sajoux took compassion on them and allowed them to live in the cell without paying rent.

The jail had been built against the wall of the old castle which rises in the center of Lourdes. In front of the spot where the jail stood there had originally been a moat. It was from this that the street got its name *Petits-Fossé* — Little Ditch. The moat had long since been filled in and covered over with cobble stones. Sajoux had his stone cutting shop on the ground floor in front. His family lived on the second floor.

The cell was at the end of a narrow unlighted hall on the ground floor. It was about eight by ten feet in size. When Sajoux had come into possession of the building, the room had but one heavily barred window, looking out on a walled-in court. Under the court flowed a drainage ditch. Sajoux had cut another window, built a fireplace, and installed a sink of slate. He had tried to rent the room, but no one would stay in it. Finally he gave up, closed one of the windows, and put a manure pile in the courtyard.

This was the room that now became the home of the Soubirous. "They were in wretched plight," says Sajoux, "more wretched than I can say. Two poor beds, one on the right of the door, the other nearer the hearth on the same side, a little old trunk containing all their linen, two chairs, a few red clay plates, and there you have the sum of their possession." There were six in the family at that time: François, Louise, Bernadette, Toinette, Jean-Marie, and Justin.

Bernadette was about twelve and a half at that time; Justin was one and a half.

Was a family ever in worse circumstances? Yet it is difficult to explain why the Soubirous should have been so unfortunate. François and Louise were both intelligent, and they got along together with no difficulty. François was not overly ambitious, but he was anxious to support his family. He took all sorts of difficult and disagreeable jobs in order to bring a little food into the house. He was not the heavy drinker that Franz Werfel has pictured him. Why, then, should this family be so poverty stricken in a community where poverty was not rampant? One is at a loss to explain it.

The Soubirous bore their misfortune with quiet resignation. They never quarreled and never complained. The children searched the alleys for rags and bones which they could sell, but they never begged. The family kept up its religious duties faithfully. Each night Andre Sajoux could hear them reciting their prayers.

Bad as things were, worse was still to come. François had been employed by Bertrand Maisongrosse, a baker, to carry bread and flour between Luz and Lourdes, a distance of twenty-five miles each way. In order to increase the small income derived from this work, he took whatever other odd jobs he could find.

One morning before daybreak, he set out to Bartes to gather faggots to sell. As he passed the wall of Dr. Dozous' garden, he noticed a plank leaning against the wall. Since it was on the public highway, he took it home.

That night the home of M. Maisongrosse was robbed of two sacks of flour. François was suspected, and his house was searched. The plank was found, and François admitted that it was not his. He denied any knowledge of the flour. He was held in jail for seven days and was finally dismissed, not because he was considered innocent, but because his guilt could not be proved. He was never cleared of the charge.

One day not long after that, Mademoiselle Estrade, a lady of the town, was praying in the church and was disturbed by the sound of chairs being moved about. Investigating the matter, she saw that they were being moved about by a small emaciated looking boy, Bernadette's brother Jean-Marie. Upon closer investigation she saw that he was scraping up and eating the wax that dripped from the candles!

In September, 1857, Marie Laguës asked Louise whether Bernadette could come to live with her and help her. She promised that Bernadette would be sent to school and would be taught her catechism. Louise readily agreed. This would be one less mouth to feed.

At Bartes, Bernadette got up every morning to help with the house before breakfast. Then she prepared breakfast for the family and lunch for herself and went out to watch the sheep until nightfall. Somehow, the promised schooling never materialized. Marie Laguës did try to teach Bernadette some catechism in the evenings, but after a hard day's work the girl found it difficult to concentrate. Sometimes Marie would box the girl's ears, throw down the book in despair, and exclaim, "Enough! You will never be anything but stupid and an ignoramus."

Bernadette longed to return to her family and was finally allowed to do so in January, 1858. She was fourteen years old by this time but looked twelve. She could neither read nor write and knew practically no Catechism. She had not yet received her first Communion.

This was the girl whom the Blessed Virgin was to select from all the people on earth for a very special mission.

CHAPTER III

THE LOURDES OF BERNADETTE

THE town to which Bernadette was so anxious to return is situated in the Pyrenees mountains in the southwestern corner of France. The Pyrenees stretch all the way from the Atlantic Ocean on the west to the Mediterranean Sea on the east, a distance of 260 miles. The great central range contains peaks of 8,000 and 9,000 feet and a few that are even higher. The boundary between France and Spain roughly follows this center range. On the French side a number of subsidiary ranges run perpendicular to the central range. The valleys lie between these smaller ranges. Picture a series of parallel valleys running north and south, and you will have grasped the principal aspect of this slope. (The Spanish slope is somewhat different, but that need not concern us.) Each valley opens onto the plain, and at each opening is a town. It can readily be understood that in bygone days these towns had great strategic value. Whoever held them held the keys to the valleys beyond. Consequently, these towns were invariably built around great rocks upon which citadels could be established. Up the valley from the fortified town there was always another town, and if the valley were long enough there was a third.

Lourdes is located near the place where the Gave de Pau leaves the mountains and enters the plain, and so it was the guardian of the valley. A citadel erected many centuries ago stands on a great rock in the center of the town. Higher up in the valley is Argeles and still farther up, almost enclosed by the towering mountains, is Luz. A short distance out on the plain is the city of Tarbes which is the capital of the Haute Pyrenees, the province in which Lourdes is located. In Bernadette's time, Tarbes was also the see of the diocese in which Lourdes was located. Still farther out on the plain is Toulouse, the unofficial capital of the French Pyrenees.

At the Atlantic end of the Pyrenees, on both the French and Spanish sides, is the race of people known as Basques. These people have their own language, customs, and dress. At the Mediterranean end are the Catalons, also a distinct race. Between these two groups there are on the Spanish side the Aragonese, and on the French side, the Bearnais. It is to the latter group that the people of Lourdes belong. The origin of these races is lost in the mists of antiquity. They have lived there since before the beginning of recorded history. Two thousand years, it is estimated, would not begin to account for the vast differences between the Catalons at one end of the chain and the Basques at the other. The Basque language bears no resemblance to any other and does not even belong to the Indo-European group.

The Bearnais, with whom we are concerned, are distinct from both the Basques and the Catalons. They are a hardy race; small, muscular, and dark. They are not bothered by the fierce heat of the summer nor by the intense cold of a Pyrenean winter. They are intelligent and lively and love a good joke. Their language is not a distinct one, as is Catalon and Basque. It is a *patois,* a combination of Spanish and French. The common headgear of the men is the Basque beret. Their greatest interest is their religion, and they have clung as tenaciously to their faith as the huts of the shepherds cling to the steep mountain sides.

The Bearnais are essentially a rural people. Those in the plain raise crops and those in the mountains raise sheep and other livestock. The rural atmosphere pervades even in the towns. In Lourdes traffic is often held up as cows, chickens, ducks, geese, and other denizens of the barnyard make their way through the streets. The French side of the mountains receives more rainfall than the Spanish side, and is consequently better farm and pasture land. The people have always been able to make a good living at their agricultural pursuits, and extreme poverty is relatively rare.

It is certain that there was a town of Lourdes long before the beginning of the Christian era. When history fails to tell us the origin of a place, legend obligingly steps in. In the time of Moses, so the story goes, there lived in Ethiopia a beautiful young princess named Tarbis. She was in love with Moses, but he rejected her hand and her throne. To forget her sorrow she gathered together a number of her subjects and wandered thousands of miles until she found herself on the bank of the Adour. The country was much to her liking, and she built a town which she called Tarbes after her own name. Her sister, who had accompanied her on her travels, went a short distance away, to where the mountains rise from the plain, and built a city called Lapurdum. From this comes the modern name of Lourdes.

Many centuries later, Caesar's lieutenant, Crassus, after a long siege, took by storm the stronghold of Lourdes. The city remained under Roman domination for five hundred years. In faraway Palestine, Christ was born and founded His Church. The new faith made its way to Rome and then to various parts of the empire, including the section known as Bearn. When the Church was persecuted by the Roman emperors, Bearn had its share of martyrs. Gradually, the entire area became Christianized and has remained so ever since.

When the Empire of the West was in the process of disintegration, the Vandals swept into southern France and laid waste the country. St. Missolinus, a priest of Tarbes, rallied the inhabitants and defeated the Vandals not far from Lourdes.

In the latter half of the fifth century, the Visigoths moved in and established the Visigothic Kingdom of Toulouse which included the southern part of France and a large section of Spain. The Visigoths, who were Arian heretics, found the

Catholic Church firmly established. They were tolerant masters, on the whole, and the Church was allowed a great amount of freedom.

Clovis, the King of the Franks, gradually extended his rule over all of northern France. When he and his followers became Catholics, he determined to drive the "heretics" out of France. After a brief but bitter campaign, he succeeded in pushing the Visigoths across the mountains into Spain. After that, Bearn became nominally a part of Clovis' kingdom, but actually it enjoyed a large degree of independence.

The Moors, who held Spain for so many centuries, spilled over into France and held Lourdes for a while. It was they who built the famous citadel. Charlemagne marched against the Moors and besieged Lourdes which was commanded by Mirat, one of the most famous leaders of Islam.

As the siege began, according to an old story, an eagle dropped a fish into the citadel. Mirat took this as an omen, because the day was Friday. He was instructed and baptized. He would not give up the fortress to anyone but the Queen of Heaven — on condition that it be held for her. For this reason, the national flag of France is lowered from the citadel once every twenty-five years. For a whole day, as a symbol of her sovereignty, the flag of the Blessed Virgin floats over the town.

One may have his doubts about the story of the fish, but in other respects the story is true. Charlemagne could not reduce the fort, and Mirat was converted. It is significant that Lourdes became a fief of our Lady more than a thousand years before her appearance at the grotto of Massabielle. Always Lourdes has been a stronghold of the faith. In the thirteenth century, the last remnants of the Albigensian heresy were overthrown beneath the walls of the historic citadel.

The history of the town during the Middle Ages is too complicated to follow. In those days, the monarchy was weak, and the nobles fought among themselves for territory. Many bloody battles took place at the citadel. Eleonora of Acquitaine, the Duke of Lancaster, the Black Prince, Simon de Montfort, and the Count of Toulouse are just a few of the rulers who held the town at various times.

For a period of forty-eight years, the British flag flew over the citadel. The Treaty of Bretigny gave Lourdes to the English. In 1408, after a siege of two years, the French won it back. This was the last time that a foreign flag was to fly over the city until the German occupation of southern France which lasted from the winter of 1942 until the summer of 1944.

At the time of the Protestant Reformation, Lourdes was the scene of several bloody encounters. The people of the region around Lourdes clung to the faith of their forefathers, but many others in southern France adopted the new religion. Much civil strife resulted. In the sixteenth century, Protestant troops besieged Lourdes but were repulsed.

Joan of Navarre, by an edict of 1562, made the district officially Protestant. When the people of Lourdes resisted the order, she set fire to the town, hoping to destroy the last vestige of Roman "impiety." The citadel, however, stood firm.

During the French Revolution, when a national madness seemed to sweep over much of France, the people of Lourdes weathered the storm with calm and patience. When priests were deported from the country, churches closed, and the Cathedral of Notre Dame converted into a "Temple of Reason," the sturdy Bearnais never wavered in their faith. They succumbed to the Revolution no more than they had to the persecution of the Roman emperors, to the Vandals, to the Arians, to the Albigensians, or to the Calvinists.

When Bernadette lived in Lourdes, it was a quaint little town. Although the valleys were well settled, the largest part of the Pyrenees had not even been explored. The forests had not been cut from the hills. Wolves, bears, and wild boars were common. With no railroad connections, Lourdes was not a buzzing metropolis. On the other hand, it would not be correct to picture it as a sleepy little country town. The population at that time was approximately five thousand. Many summer resorts were located in the district, and, all summer long, wealthy people passed through Lourdes in carriages. Many of them stayed in the town overnight. On certain days, the fairs and markets brought crowds to Lourdes. The principal street of the town at times resembled the boulevard of a large city.

Several government officials were stationed in Lourdes, and a law court was located there. A platoon of infantry was housed in the ancient citadel, and two or three companies of cavalry occupied a district a few hundred yards from the city. The town had a hospital and six surgeons. It had a newspaper of its own, and Paris papers were received regularly. There were several fine schools which were well attended. The boys went to school to some lay institution or to the school conducted by the Brothers. The girls went to the school conducted by the Sisters of Nevers. The children received a better education than most of those in the large cities at that time.

The people really lived their religion. There were eight beneficial societies which dated from the Middle Ages. These societies were based on sound Christian principles and were under the patronage of Our Lady of Mount Carmel, Our Lady of Mount Serrat, Our Lady of Grace, St. Lucy, St. Anne, the Blessed Sacrament, The Ascension, and SS. John and James. The women had a religious association called the Congregation of the Children of Mary. To obtain admission, the candidate had to be of irreproachable character. It was considered an honor to be admitted to the society, and exclusion was a great disgrace. Little girls looked forward to the day when they would be old enough to enter it.

In speaking of the deep religious convictions of the people, certain exceptions should be noted. The government officials and other members of the "intelligentsia" were imbued with the indifferentism which was characteristic of the age and which was a carryover from the French Revolution.

These people were in the minority, but they were in positions of authority and were to cause a great deal of trouble.

Most of the town in Bernadette's time was on the slope of the hill between the foot of the citadel and the river. The cobblestone streets were steep and narrow. The majority of the houses were simple little cottages, and the shops were very small. The town presented a very different appearance from the Lourdes of today with its many large hotels and its souvenir shops. The cobblestone streets, however, still remain to keep in the town an air of quaintness.

Across the river and west of the town stands the rock of Massabielle. In order to reach it, one left the town by the rue de Barons (now the rue de la Grotte) and passed through an ancient gate which had once belonged to the castle. A steep, stony road led to the bank of the river, the Gave du Pau. A stone bridge, the Pont Vieux, led to the opposite bank. Here, one turned slightly to the right and followed a narrow, tortuous path which bordered the field of Monsieur de la Fitte. Upon reaching the hill of Massabielle, one could cross a little mill stream at the Mill of Savy, cross the end of La Fitte's field, and find oneself across the stream from the rock. Or upon reaching the hill, one could climb it and come down the other side and also be at the rock. Bernadette and her companions took the first route the day they set out to gather wood. They returned by the other route.

All this is assuming that one had any desire to reach Massabielle. Such a thing would be unlikely. The region was wild, difficult to reach, and had a bad reputation. Bernadette and her companions came across it by accident, not by intention.

Here at the rock of Massabielle, the mill stream joins the Gave, which takes a right angle turn after leaving Lourdes. The rock is pierced by three irregular caverns, one above the other and all interconnected. The first and largest of these caverns is level with the ground. The entrance is a misshapen arch about fifteen feet high and the cavern is about forty feet wide and forty feet deep. Above and to the right are the two smaller openings, the largest of which is about the size of a niche in a church. When Bernadette went to Massabielle, the rock; its branches trailed to the foot of this opening. The there was an eglantine, or wild rose, growing from a crack in caverns were called the grotto of Massabielle, which in the dialect of the country means Old Rocks.

It is thought that many centuries ago, the grotto was used by a devil-worshiping sect and that many human sacrifices were offered there. This story accounts in part for the bad name which the region had with the deeply religious people of Lourdes. If true, the devil probably looked upon this as his domain and was doubly resentful when our Lady decided to make it her own.

The grotto and near-by land was owned by the city of Lourdes. The poor of the town often brought their pigs there to feed. In case of rain, the cavern served as a shelter. Fishermen used it sometimes as a place to dry their nets. Aside from these few people, the region was rarely visited.

Again, we see how little our Lady is guided by earthly standards. Of all the regions in the Pyrenees, Massabielle would seem to be the least likely for her to hallow by her presence.

Chapter IV

BERNADETTE AND THE LADY

BERNADETTE returned to Lourdes and took up her residence in the cachot in January, 1858. The First Apparition took place on February 11, just a few weeks later. This is the story in the girl's own words:

"The Thursday before Ash Wednesday it was cold, and the weather was threatening. After our dinner, my mother told us that there was no more wood in the house and she was vexed. My sister Toinette and I, to please her, offered to go and pick up dry branches by the riverside. My mother said, 'No,' because the weather was bad and we might be in danger of falling into the Gave. Jeanne Abadie, our neighbor and friend, who was looking after her little brother in our house and who wanted to come with us, took her brother back to his house and returned the next moment telling us that she had leave to come with us. My mother still hesitated, but seeing that there were three of us she let us go. We took first of all the road which leads to the cemetery, by the side of which wood is unloaded and where shavings can sometimes be found. That day we found nothing there. We came down by the side which leads near the Gave and having arrived at Pont Vieux we wondered if it would be best to go up or down the river. We decided to go down and taking the forest road we arrived at Merlasse. There we went into Monsieur de la Fitte's field by the mill of Savy. As soon as we had reached the end of the field, nearly opposite the grotto of Massabielle, we were stopped by the canal of the mill we had just passed. The current of this canal was not strong for the mill was not working, but the water was cold and I for my part was afraid to go in. Jeanne Abadie and my sister, less timid than I, took their sabots in their hands and crossed the stream. However, when they were on the other side they called out that it was cold and bent down to rub their feet and warm them. All this increased my fear, and I thought that if I went into the water, I should get an attack of asthma. So I asked Jeanne Abadie, who was bigger and stronger than I, to take me on her shoulders.

" 'I should think not,' answered Jeanne; 'you're a mollycoddle; if you won't come, stay where you are.'

"After the others had picked up some pieces of wood under the grotto, they disappeared along the Gave. When I was alone, I threw some stones into the bed of the stream to give me a foothold, but it was of no use. So I had to make up my mind to take off my sabots and cross the canal as Jeanne and my sister had done.

"I had just begun to take off my first stocking when suddenly I heard a great noise like the sound of a storm. I looked to the right, to the left, under the trees of the river, but nothing moved; I thought I was mistaken. I went on taking off my shoes and stockings, when I heard a fresh noise like the first. Then I was frightened and stood straight up. I lost all power of speech and thought when, turning my head toward the grotto, I saw at one of the openings of the rock a bush, one only, moving as if it were very windy. Almost at the same time there came out of the interior of the grotto a golden colored cloud, and soon after a Lady, young and beautiful, exceedingly beautiful, the like of whom I had never seen, came and placed herself at the entrance of the opening above the bush. She looked at me immediately, smiled at me and signed me to advance, as if she had been my mother. All fear had left me, but I seemed to know no longer where I was. I rubbed my eyes, I shut them, I opened them; but the Lady was still there continuing to smile at me and making me understand that I was not mistaken. Without thinking of what I was doing, I took my rosary in my hands

Bernadette

A view of Lourdes

— Philip Gendreau

The Railroad Station at Lourdes

**Crowd gathering for the Blessing of the Sick. This photograph was taken
on a rainy day — notice the hoods on the wheelchairs**

Pilgrims in the streets of Lourdes

and went on my knees. The Lady made with her head a sign
of approval and herself took into her hands a rosary which
hung on her right arm. When I attempted to begin the rosary
and tried to lift my hand to my forehead, my arm remained
paralyzed, and it was only after the Lady had signed herself
that I could do the same. The Lady left me to pray all alone;
she passed the beads of her rosary between her fingers but
she said nothing; only at the end of each decade did she say
the 'Gloria' with me.

"When the recitation of the rosary was finished, the Lady
returned to the interior of the rock and the golden cloud
disappeared with her."

At this point, the listener usually stopped Bernadette to ask
her what the Lady looked like. She would reply:

"She has the appearance of a young girl of sixteen or
seventeen. She is dressed in a white robe, girdled at the waist
with a blue ribbon which flows down all along her robe. She
wears upon her head a veil which is also white; this veil gives
just a glimpse of her hair and then falls down at the back
below her waist. Her feet are bare but covered by the last
folds of her robe except at the point where a yellow rose
shines upon each of them. She holds on her right arm a rosary
of white beads with a chain of gold shining like the two roses
on her feet."

Shortly after the Lady had disappeared, Jeanne and
Toinette returned to the grotto and found Bernadette still on
her knees. They laughed at her and asked her if she were
going back with them. She waded into the stream and said,
"The water is not so cold as you would have me believe."

The girls bound up their wood into little bundles and
climbed the hill of Massabielle. As they were walking home,
Bernadette asked her two companions whether they had
noticed anything unusual at the grotto.

"No. Why do you ask us?"

"Oh, nothing," replied Bernadette with pretended in-
difference.

Before they got to the house, however, Bernadette told her sister of the extraordinary occurrence at the grotto. She asked her sister not to tell it.

The image of the Lady remained in Bernadette's mind the whole day. While the family was saying its prayers that night, the girl began to cry.

"What is the matter?" asked her mother.

Toinette told what had happened at the grotto, and then Bernadette was obliged to relate the entire story.

"These are illusions," said Louise Soubirous. "You must get these ideas out of your head, and you must not go back to Massabielle."

That night the girl could not sleep. The face of the Lady kept returning to her. She could not believe that the event had been an illusion.

In obedience to the command of her mother, Bernadette stayed away from the grotto for the next two days. On Sunday, however, a number of her classmates begged her mother to allow her to go back. Finally, Louise consented. Many persons had suggested that the vision might be diabolical, so Bernadette took a bottle of holy water with her.

At the grotto the girls knelt down while Bernadette said her Rosary. Just as she was completing the fifth decade, the Lady appeared again. Only Bernadette could see her. The children who had accompanied her could see nothing but an ugly black hole. When Bernadette threw some holy water at her, the Lady smiled approvingly. A short time later Bernadette seemed to go into a trance. The girls were terrified. They feared she was dead. Several of them ran to get Antoine Nicolau, the miller. He and the others got the girl to her feet and pulled her along the path to the mill. There, after a short time, her consciousness returned.

"I saw a very beautiful girl," Bernadette cried, "and she had her hands joined."

In great excitement she showed how the girl had held her

hands. As she talked, the color returned to her face, and she resumed her natural appearance.

"Never have I seen a more marvelous sight," said Nicolau of Bernadette in her trance. "I felt that I was not worthy to touch the child."

The Third Apparition took place Thursday, February 18. Someone had told Bernadette to take pen, ink, and paper and ask the Lady to write her message. When the girl did so, the Lady spoke for the first time.

"There is no need to write what I have to say."

Then she said, "Will you do me the kindness of coming here for two weeks?"

"I will come. I will ask my parents' permission," Bernadette answered.

The Lady then said to her, "I do not promise to make you happy in this world, but in the other."

The following day Bernadette's aunt, her mother, and many others accompanied her to the grotto. The child had scarcely begun to say the rosary when the Lady appeared. Bernadette's face became transfigured. This was the first time Louise had been present at any of the visions, and she became frightened when she saw her daughter in such a state.

By this time, the story of the apparitions had spread throughout the countryside. When Bernadette reached the grotto on Saturday, she found that a large crowd was already gathered. The banks of the river were lined with curious people. They even climbed the rock of Massabielle itself.

Bernadette seemed not to see the crowd as she knelt on the large smooth stone that was always saved for her. She gazed in rapture at the niche which seemed empty to the other people. Sometimes she smiled, and sometimes her eyes filled with tears. She and the Lady talked together and prayed together, but the people could hear nothing. Some of the things that the Lady told Bernadette during her visits were for her ears alone and were never repeated.

The sixth visit took place on Sunday. Bernadette set out at six o'clock in the morning, but even then the crowd was enormous. She made her way through the jostling throng to her usual place.

Present at this visit was a physician of Lourdes, Dr. Dozous. The doctor did not believe in supernatural visions and had come "to put an end to this nonsense."

On this day, great tears ran down Bernadette's cheeks. The Lady looked very sad, and she said, "Pray for sinners." Very quickly, however, she smiled again, and Bernadette's heart overflowed with happiness.

Dr. Dozous watched the girl very closely. He was ready to call her a fraud or a person who was mentally deranged. The tears puzzled him. They were real enough. And the expression on the girl's face! She would have to be the most wonderful actress the world had ever known in order to simulate that. He took her pulse. It was normal.

When the vision was over, Dr. Dozous asked Bernadette many questions. She gave full, straightforward answers, and never once did she hesitate or contradict herself. She gave no evidence of being insane.

The doctor, who had come to "expose" Bernadette, decided to reserve judgment.

The local officials were becoming apprehensive about the large crowds that were gathering at the grotto. The officials did not believe in the visions, but it was plain that the crowds did. If the people could be duped so easily, who could tell what might happen next? This thing must be stopped.

The first official to deal with Bernadette was M. Dutour, the imperial prosecutor. He called Bernadette to his office on February 21, just after the Sixth Apparition. He tried to convince Bernadette that her Lady was purely imaginary, but the girl would not be swayed from her story. Then he accused Bernadette of making a good thing of her so-called visions and asked her if it wasn't true that her parents had received gifts privately. She replied that they had not received gifts from anyone. Dutour, seeing that he was not getting any place, dismissed the girl.

The police commissioner, M. Jacomet, questioned Bernadette the same day. He was an old hand at getting confessions from criminals, and he was sure this fourteen-year-old girl would be easy prey. J. B. Estrade, a tax collector, who was stationed at Lourdes, lived in the same house with Jacomet. Out of curiosity, he stepped into the room in which the police commissioner was questioning the girl and took a chair.

At first, Jacomet used the strategy of kindness. In a very fatherly way, he asked the girl to admit that her visions were not real. In this he had no more success than Dutour had had earlier in the day. Next, he took down her story on paper and then read it back to her, intentionally making many mistakes. She corrected every mistake.

Jacomet then threatened Bernadette. He told her that she must stay away from the grotto or he would put her into prison. Bernadette replied that she could not stay away, because she had promised the Lady that she would come.

François Soubirous came rushing into the room. He had been worried about his daughter and had come to see what was going on. Jacomet advised François to forbid his daughter to visit the grotto. François readily agreed to do so. He had already been in trouble with the police and wanted no more difficulty with them.

When the father and daughter had left, Estrade and Jacomet discussed the case. The police commissioner was convinced that the girl was a fraud.

"No," said Estrade, "she is sincere. Do you think a poor peasant girl could recite a made-up story in such a way and with such earnestness? It is impossible."

Estrade still did not believe in the reality of the apparitions. He could see though that the girl herself did believe in them. In due time, he was to become completely convinced that her story was true and was to become one of her strongest supporters.

Poor Bernadette had promised the Lady that she would come to the grotto every day for two weeks! Now her father had forbidden her to go. The next day, Monday, February 22, she took her spelling book and went off to school. At noon, she came home to a meal of black bread and then started off to the afternoon session.

When she reached the crossroads, an invisible barrier stopped her. Try as she would, she could not go on. Then something within her, a voice she could not disobey, bade her go to the grotto. Some police, seeing her on the way to Massabielle, followed her. So did a number of other persons including Estrade's sister.

But the Lady did not appear that day.

Those who had scoffed at the story all along did not fail to make capital of this. "Jacomet and his police have frightened the Lady away," they said.

After the incident of the invisible barrier, Bernadette's father no longer forbade the girl to go to the grotto.

The next day the Lady was back. A number of men from Lourdes, among whom was Estrade, stood silently while the ecstasy lasted — more than an hour this time. They had come to scoff, but they were deeply impressed by the transfiguration of Bernadette's features, her Signs of the Cross, and the amazing influence that spread from her. What the Lady said that day was for Bernadette's ears alone.

Four or five hundred persons were on hand for the Eighth Apparition on Wednesday, February 24. Estrade was not there that day, but his sister was. She tells us that Bernadette wept bitterly and advanced on her knees to the place where the wild rose bush was hanging, prostrating herself at each step. Then she turned to the people and said, "Penitence! Penitence! Penitence!" Mlle. Estrade was too far away to hear this herself, but she reported what others told her.

A soldier pushed his way through the crowd and stood at Bernadette's side. "What are you doing, you little actress?" he said. Bernadette, lost in the vision, paid no attention. The soldier then turned to the crowd and cried, "And to think that such follies can take place in the nineteenth century!"

The crowd became hostile and murmured against the soldier. Nearly everyone present believed in Bernadette by this time and would tolerate no interference. When the soldier saw the temper of the crowd, he quickly withdrew.

During the Ninth Apparition, on February 25, the Lady said to Bernadette, "Go, drink and wash in the spring."

But Bernadette could see no spring.

Estrade, who was present at this scene, describes it thus: "At the end of some moments, the seer got up once more and seemed embarrassed; hesitating, she turned away toward the Gave and took two or three steps toward it. Suddenly, she stopped abruptly, looked behind her as though hearing herself called, and listened to words which seemed to come to her from the side of the rock. She made a sign of assent, began to walk once more, but toward the grotto this time, not toward the Gave, to the left corner of the excavations. After having gone about three-quarters of the way, she stopped and cast a troubled look around. She raised her head as though to question the Lady; then she resolutely bent down and began to scratch the earth. The little cavity which she hollowed out became full of muddy water; after having waited a moment she drank of it and washed her face; she also took a blade of grass which grew on the soil and raised it to her mouth. All the spectators followed the phases of this strange scene with a painful feeling and a sort of stupor. When the child raised herself to return to her place, her face was still smeared with muddy water. Seeing this a cry of disappointment and pity rose from the lips of all: 'Bernadette is out of her mind! The poor child has become insane!'

"Bernadette returned to her place without seeming moved and even without taking any notice of the exclamations sounding in her ears. After her face had been cleaned, she resumed her contemplation of the heavenly vision, happier than ever, and with an angelic smile upon her lips."

Those who had sneered at the visions were louder than ever in their ridicule now. "She is deranged," these people said. "Isn't that what we have been telling you?"

Those who had believed in the girl were disappointed and bewildered. Most of them went home in silence, but some were bitter in their denunciation of the girl who had "made fools" of them.

The disappointment of Bernadette's followers was not to last for long. Water began trickling from the little cavity which the girl had scooped out. The trickle grew larger and larger. Almost immediately miraculous cures were said to have taken place by means of the water. The enthusiasm of Bernadette's followers became greater than ever.

For a time it was widely believed that this spring had a miraculous origin, that it had sprung up from the dry floor of the grotto at the Lady's bidding. The evidence does not support this story. There had always been a spring near the mouth of the grotto, but it was often covered over by the debris which the river had deposited there. At such times the water came to the surface farther back in the cave, where Bernadette found it. Today with the floor of the grotto cleared, the water flows from the front. The spring was miraculously revealed to Bernadette, and the wonders that are accomplished through its use are miraculous. Its origin, however, is as natural as that of myriads of other springs in the Pyrenees.

On Friday, February 26, the Lady said to Bernadette, "Bend low and kiss the ground for the sake of sinners." Bernadette did so, and all the people present did likewise. The Eleventh Apparition, on the next day, passed without any unusual event taking place, and so did the Twelfth on Sunday.

Before the Thirteenth Apparition, a friend asked Bernadette to use her rosary that day. The girl consented, but had scarcely begun her prayers when the Lady stopped her. Bernadette took her own rosary out of her pocket and nodded as if in answer to a question. The crowd, seeing Bernadette hold out her rosary to ask if it was the one she should use, thought the Lady was blessing rosaries. They held theirs out. Some of the French newspapers seized upon this incident and jeered at the "silly proceedings" which were taking place at Lourdes.

On March 2, the Lady asked Bernadette to tell the priests that she wished a chapel built at Massabielle and that she wished processions to come there. This taxed Bernadette's courage to the utmost; she was afraid of the Abbé Peyramale who was her pastor and also the Dean of Lourdes. But she had to do what the Lady had requested.

The Abbé had maintained an aloof attitude during the entire proceedings at the grotto and had ordered the priests under his jurisdiction to do likewise. Now, he found himself face to face with the girl who was creating all the excitement. He looked at her sternly, as the girl in a trembling voice repeated the Lady's request.

"Ask the Lady," said Abbé Peyramale, "to make the rose-bush at the grotto blossom at once before the assembled crowd, and then I will be her humble servant."

The vision of March 3 is omitted from many accounts, but there can be no doubt that it took place. This brings the total number of apparitions to nineteen instead of eighteen, the number that is usually given. Bernadette went to the grotto about seven o'clock in the morning. Four thousand persons were there. Many of them had been there all night. The Lady did not appear, and Bernadette was grief stricken. The disappointed crowd dispersed. About nine o'clock Bernadette returned to the grotto and found the Lady waiting for her. It was the only time this happened. Later, Bernadette reported to Abbé Peyramale.

"The Lady smiled when I told her that you wanted her to make the rosebush bloom. She smiled once more and said she wanted a chapel."

"Have you any money?" the Abbé asked angrily.

"No, Monsieur le Curé!"

"Neither have I! Go tell your Lady to give you some!"

The next day was the last day of the two weeks. More than 20,000 persons were at the grotto. They came on foot and on horseback and in every kind of conveyance they could secure. They crowded the streets of the village to such an extent that the police had to call upon the troops to help maintain order.

The Lady appeared, but nothing noteworthy happened. When she disappeared, Bernadette did not know whether she should ever see her again.

For three weeks there were no more visions. The people of the region continued to visit the grotto, and they kept candles burning there all the time. They bathed in the water of the spring, and they began collecting money with which to build a church. The civil officials were angry because they thought the entire world was laughing at them. The Church authorities continued to hold aloof, believing that if the manifestations were really miraculous, nothing would prevent God's will from being fulfilled.

March 25 was the Feast of the Annunciation. On the eve of that day, Bernadette felt a call to the grotto. She went at dawn.

Until this time, Bernadette had always referred to her visitor as "the Lady." Others had freely called her the Blessed Virgin, but when Bernadette was questioned on the matter, she always said, "I don't know who she is."

Let us hear in the girl's own words what took place at the Seventeenth Apparition.

"When I was on my knees before the Lady, I asked her pardon for arriving late. Always good and gracious, she made a sign to me that I need not excuse myself. Then I spoke to her of all my affection, all my respect, and the happiness I had in seeing her again. After having poured out my heart to her, I took up my rosary. Whilst I was praying, the thought of asking her name came before my mind with such persistence that I could think of nothing else. I feared to be presumptuous in repeating a question she had always refused to answer, and yet something compelled me to speak. At last, under an irresistible impulse, the words fell from my mouth, and I begged the Lady to tell me who she was. The Lady did as she had always done before; she bowed her head and smiled and did not reply. I cannot say why, but I felt myself bolder and asked her again to graciously tell me her name; however she only bowed and smiled as before, still remaining silent. Then once more, for the third time, clasping my hands and confessing myself unworthy of the favor I was asking of her, I again made my request.

"The Lady was standing above the rosebush, in a position very similar to that shown on the miraculous medal. At my third request, her face became very serious, and she seemed to bow down in an attitude of humility. Then she joined her hands and raised them to her breast. She looked up to heaven. Then slowly opening her hands and leaning forward towards me, she said to me in a voice vibrating with emotion,

" 'I AM THE IMMACULATE CONCEPTION.' "

Bernadette did not know what these words meant. She repeated them over and over as she went to Abbé Peyramale to tell him what the Lady had said. The Abbé was puzzled and distressed. He still could not bring himself to believe Bernadette's story, but his disbelief was wavering. The girl could not have invented that statement.

The people, naturally, were wild with joy. They had believed all along that the Lady was the Blessed Virgin, and now she had confirmed their belief.

The civil authorities were as far from being convinced as ever. They had a committee of doctors examine Bernadette in the hope that they would declare her insane and have her sent away. After innumerable questions, the doctors reported that the girl seemed perfectly well balanced.

On April 7, Bernadette went to the grotto once more, and a number of people went with her. Among them was Dr. Dozous. The Lady appeared for the eighteenth time that day.

Dr. Dozous knelt near the child and watched her closely. In her hand, as was her custom, she carried a lighted candle. Her face became radiant with ecstasy. Her fingers accidentally came in contact with the flame of the candle several times. The amazed Dr. Dozous saw that the flame had no effect upon her skin. After the vision was over, the doctor held a flame near the girl's hand.

"Oh, be careful!" she cried. "You are burning me."

This incident has been greatly exaggerated in various accounts. Some stories have it that Bernadette's hand remained in the flame for fifteen minutes. Père Cros, who is the best authority upon Lourdes and the apparitions, doubts that there was anything miraculous about the occurrence. It was enough, however, to bring about the complete conversion of Dr. Dozous.

The authorities decided that it was time to act. Jacomet and his police cleared the grotto of all articles of devotion and forbade the people to gather there for public worship. The people ignored the orders. Several more miraculous cures took place at the spring.

The prefect of the district, Baron Massy, ordered the Mayor to have a fence built around the grotto. Several policemen were put on guard to see that no one broke down the fence. The Baron also sent away a sample of the water to a chemist. He was sure that an analysis of the water would show that it had some healing power. The cures had to be explained in some way.

On June 3, the Feast of Corpus Christi, Bernadette received her first Holy Communion. She had been preparing for this event ever since her return to Lourdes in January.

On July 16, Bernadette felt a strong desire to go to the grotto. Because of the fence that had been built around it, she was forced to take her place across the river from the scene of the visions. The Blessed Virgin appeared to her once more. The Lady smiled a tender farewell and then disappeared — never to return.

The report from the chemist was a great disappointment to the prefect. After a complete chemical analysis, the chemist reported that the water was essentially the same as that of other springs of the neighborhood and had no medicinal qualities. The prefect still stubbornly said that the grotto must be kept closed. Meanwhile people were contriving to get to the grotto despite the police and the fence. Many offenders were taken into court and fined. The priests begged the people not to resort to violence.

The inhabitants of Lourdes protested to the Emperor, Napoleon III, who was vacationing at Biarritz not far away. To their great delight, the Emperor ordered that the grotto be opened at once. Upon instructions from the prefect, Mayor Lacade issued a proclamation declaring that the barriers would be removed and everyone was free to visit the grotto.

A great crowd rushed joyously to Massabielle, tore down the fences, and knelt to give thanks to the Blessed Virgin.

Peace descended on the town of Lourdes.

Chapter V

HAPPINESS DEFERRED

"I DO not promise to make you happy in this life but in the other," the Lady had said to Bernadette.

Bernadette's life after the apparitions was certainly far from happy. She suffered extreme mental and physical anguish. Perhaps the hardest thing to bear was that never again could she go her way without attracting attention. After being selected by God to see His Mother, she could never hope to lead a normal life. Yet she bore her sufferings with great fortitude. No doubt the memory of the Virgin at Massabielle helped her through the trying years. The Lady's promise was probably a great consolation.

François Soubirous, with the help of Abbé Peyramale, obtained another mill on the Lapaca near the point where this stream emptied into the Gave. The mill was rather run down, and François still was not a good businessman. He had enough business, however, to keep his family from ever again being poverty stricken. No doubt, Bernadette's fame brought customers to the mill.

Bernadette lived at this mill for about a year and a half. During the day, she went to school at the Hospice which was run by the Sisters of Charity and Christian Instruction of Nevers. In the evenings, she helped her mother with the housework and with the care of the younger children. A baby brother, Bernard-Pierre, was born September 10, 1859.

Soon after the apparitions, Bernadette expressed the desire to become a nun. She wished to be a Carmelite, but her health was not good enough for her to be admitted to that order.

The girl's life was not her own. Pilgrims were beginning to come to Lourdes in large numbers, and all of them tried to see Bernadette. She felt that she was constantly on display "like some kind of animal." It was partly because of this fact that Abbé Peyramale suggested that she should lead a more secluded life. He arranged for her to go and live with the Sisters at the Hospice. She took up her residence in the Hospice in January, 1860; she was then sixteen years old. She helped in the kitchens, the workroom, and the infirmary.

The change in residence did not bring about the desired privacy. No matter what Bernadette was doing the bell would ring, and she would be called away to tell visitors the detailed story of the apparitions. She did this so often that sometimes her eyes would fill with tears at the thought of going through the ordeal once more. When she met the visitors, however, she would be very gracious. She had been taking lessons in French, and was soon able to talk with the visitors without the aid of an interpreter.

Abbé Peyramale wanted to protect Bernadette from being constantly interviewed, but the Sisters usually found it hard to refuse the visitors' requests. They had come such a long distance, and they did want to see Bernadette "just this once." Some of the visitors were very distinguished. Not a few of them were Bishops. How could a Sister refuse the request of a Bishop?

Many of those who interviewed Bernadette were curious about the secrets which the Lady had told her, but the girl refused to divulge any information on this point.

"Would you tell the secrets to the Pope?" Bernadette heard this question over and over.

"No."

"But the Pope is the Vicar of Christ."

"The Pope is very powerful on earth, but the Blessed Virgin is powerful in heaven."

The interviews fatigued Bernadette and aggravated her already bad health. One day, in 1862, her condition became so bad that she was given the Last Sacraments. Later, she recovered to the point where she could again go about her tasks.

In September of that year, a baby, who had been born to Bernadette's mother in February, died. He had never been strong.

Later that month, Bishop Forcade of Nevers, where the mother house of the Sisters of the Hospice was located, came to visit the Hospice. During his tour of inspection, he came across Bernadette grating carrots in the kitchen. That evening he sent for her and asked her what she intended to do with herself.

"Nothing," was the answer.

"My dear child, you must do something in the world."

"I am quite content here with these good Sisters."

"But you can't remain here always. They only took you for a time out of charity."

"Why can't I stay here always?"

"Because you are not a Sister."

"I don't think I should do for a Sister. I have no dowry, and I cannot do anything."

"You need not worry about the dowry, and I think you underestimate your talents. You are good at something."

"Good for what?"

"This morning I saw you grating carrots."

Bernadette promised to think the matter over. Some time later, she asked to be admitted to the novitiate. Her entrance was put off for two more years because of her extremely bad health.

Early in 1865, Bernadette's ten-year-old brother Justin died. There is no record as to what caused the death of the Soubirous children, and their mother and father a little later, but it is certain that they had been exposed to Bernadette's tuberculosis.

Bernadette was to leave for the mother house at Nevers on July 4, 1866. Her mother, father, godmother, and some others

came to the Hospice the evening before. Her mother was
very ill, but not too ill to visit her daughter.

The next day Bernadette said good-by to the grotto. She
was almost overcome with emotion. She tried to say the rosary
but couldn't do so. Prostrating herself on the ground, she cried,
"O Mother, my Mother, how can I leave you?"

She stopped for a few moments at the mill. The family
gathered in silence. No one could say anything. Bernadette
clasped them, kissed them, and then rushed out to the waiting
carriage. With two brief exceptions, she was never to see any
of them again.

All the first day at the mother house, Bernadette wept with
homesickness. Later, she always went out of her way to
comfort girls who were entering the convent. She never forgot
her own homesickness that first day.

On July 27, 1866, Bernadette put on the habit of the Sisters
of Charity and took the name Sister Marie-Bernard. This, it
will be remembered, was her baptismal name. Three weeks
is a short time for a postulancy, but her years at the Hospice
were taken into consideration.

Soon after this, the Mother Superior called together the
entire convent and had Bernadette tell the story of her
apparitions. When she had finished, the Mother Superior told
the Sisters that the apparitions must never be referred to
again. This must have pleased Bernadette. She longed for
nothing so much as to be left in peace. The Sisters adhered
to the rule, but streams of distinguished visitors kept coming
to the convent door. As was the case at the Hospice, the
Mother Superior could not refuse them permission to interview
Bernadette — so the ordeal went on.

The Mother Superior was Mother Josephine Imbert. Her
assistant, and mistress of novices, Mother Marie-Thérèse
Vauzous, was said to have had "a veritable passion for the
fashioning of souls." She was the daughter of a French general
and had been taught the strictest type of discipline for as long
a time as she could remember.

Both these good Sisters had the idea that Bernadette needed humbling. She had received so much adulation from the world that it seemed inconceivable that some of it had not gone to her head. They could not realize that Bernadette detested this adulation from the bottom of her heart, and wanted more than anything else to get far away from it. It is impossible to tell how much Bernadette suffered because her superiors were of this opinion. Biographers do not agree on this point. Even the Sisters who were in the convent at the time did not agree. That she suffered to some extent is beyond doubt.

In Bernadette's diary we find such entries as, "When I suffer from the contempt of my superiors or my companions, when I bleed from the humiliations that they inflict upon me, I must never fail immediately to offer thanks to our Lord."

One of the other young nuns remembered saying, "What a mercy I am not Bernadette."

Mother Marie-Thérèse herself, toward the end of her life, doubted her own wisdom in her handling of Bernadette. She said she was astounded at her own harshness and even uneasy about it.

Bernadette never complained. When asked if she minded the treatment of Mother Marie-Thérèse, she would say, "The novice mistress knows what she is about. I do have lots of pride."

In the latter part of October, 1866, Bernadette seemed at the point of death. The Last Sacraments were again administered, and Bishop Forcade came to the convent and gave her the vows of the order. She was now a full-fledged member of the community.

On the Feast of the Immaculate Conception, Louise Soubirous died. The death of her mother was a great blow to Bernadette. She had not seen her mother since that day in the kitchen at the mill.

On October 30, 1867, Bernadette made her profession again with the other girls of the novitiate. The young nuns were then given letters assigning them to various houses of the order. It had previously been agreed that Bernadette would be allowed to stay at Nevers, in order to protect her from the eyes of the curious. Bishop Forcade, who assigned the letters, later said that "the wisdom of Mother Josephine knew how to make even this privilege an humiliation."

"Why," asked the Bishop, "do I have no letter of obedience for Sister Marie-Bernard?"

"Monseigneur," said Mother Josephine, "it has not been possible to assign her an obedience. She is good for nothing."

The Bishop called Bernadette. She knelt before him.

"You aren't good for anything? But my poor child, what are we going to do with you? And what good is your entry into the congregation?"

"That is just what I told you at Lourdes, my lord, and you answered that it would not make any difference."

The Mother Superior broke in.

"If you like, Monseigneur, we can keep her out of charity and employ her in the infirmary. As she is almost always sick, it will be just the place for her. She can begin by keeping it clean, and if we are able to teach her, perhaps she will be able to make up cough mixtures later on."

Bernadette admitted, some time later, that this public humiliation was very bitter to her. At the time, she did not allow her emotion to show.

Cleaning a sickroom is very disagreeable work, but Bernadette entered upon it without making the least complaint. After some years she was, at the doctor's orders, transferred to the sacristy to be undersacristan. She retained this post till her death.

In 1870 came the Franco-Prussian War. Not much is known about Bernadette's life during this period. In her letters home, she said that France was being punished for its sins.

"They say," she wrote, "that the enemy is approaching the gate of Nevers. I could get along very well without seeing the Prussians, but I am not afraid of them. God is everywhere."

The enemy did come very close to Nevers. Bishop Forcade

moved most of the younger sisters to other houses, but Bernadette was left at the mother house.

In 1871, François Soubirous died, and Bernadette, being
the oldest child, became the nominal head of the family.

Bernadette never regarded herself as a saint, but practically
everyone around her did, and this was the source of a great
amount of anguish to her. Everyone wanted to touch her or
be touched by her. Anything that she handled was regarded
as a relic. People were constantly handing her all sorts of
objects so she would hand them back. One day, she distributed
some coated almonds to some visiting children. As soon as
the children left the room their elders took the candy away
from them, so they could keep it for a souvenir. When Bernadette worked in the linen room, every scrap that fell from
her scissors was picked up and treasured. Every time her
hair was cut, all the hair that fell to the floor was gathered
up and kept. The other Sisters tried to touch her robe or
kiss her veil every time she passed. They tried to walk next
to her when she was coming down the stairs. They tried to
work with her in the infirmary. They even wanted to get sick
so that they would be under her care in the infirmary.

All of this was extremely trying to Bernadette, especially
in view of the fact that she was suffering such intense physical
pain at the same time. The superiors, seeing all this adulation,
were more strongly confirmed in their opinion that Bernadette
needed humbling for the salvation of her soul.

Her pain was becoming almost unendurable. Her chest
became more and more feeble. A large tumor formed on her
knee. Her bones were rotting away. Today, a person with
tuberculosis is given complete rest, but, at that time, not
very much was known about the treatment of the disease.
Bernadette's work probably aggravated her condition.

It is recorded that at times Bernadette was rather short-
tempered, and no wonder! On the whole, however, she
endured her agonies with almost superhuman fortitude. When
she was really ill and confined to bed, she was very good

tempered. She worked contentedly on little pieces of embroidery, and she scraped tiny designs on egg shells. She became very adept at both kinds of work. Perhaps she was more good natured when she was sick enough to stay in bed, because at such times she was better protected from those who venerated her.

In March, 1878, Mother Josephine Imbert died, and Mother Marie-Thérèse Vauzous was transferred. Bernadette's last months were free from the efforts of these two to see that she remained humble. The new superior, Mother Adelaide Dons, did not feel that it was necessary to humble Bernadette. She did everything in her power to make Bernadette's life a little more bearable.

On September 22, 1878, Bernadette made her perpetual and final vows.

In October, her brother Jean-Marie came for a brief visit. The two were overjoyed at seeing each other after so long a time.

On December 12, when she again seemed at the point of death, the bishops of Tarbes and Nevers asked her to repeat the long story of the apparitions.

The following March 19, her sister, Toinette, who had been with her the day of the First Apparition, came to see her. There is no record of their conversation.

During Holy Week, her suffering became more intense. Easter brought no relief. Tuesday night, she sank into a half stupor from which she roused at times to cry in terror, "Begone, Satan! Get thee hence, Satan! Begone!"

In the morning, she could no longer breathe lying down. She was placed in a chair. The Sisters knelt around her and recited the prayers for the dying. She clutched a crucifix to her breast.

After a time, she raised herself in her chair and asked for water. Her lips were moistened. She made the Sign of the Cross. Then she sank back. "Blessed Mary, Mother of God, pray for me! — a poor sinner, a poor sinner . . . " she mur-

mured. She bowed her head in death. It was about three
o'clock in the afternoon, April 16, 1879.

"I do not promise to make you happy in this life but in
the other," the Lady had said.

Bernadette, after all her suffering, had gone to claim the
unutterable happiness of heaven that her Lady had promised
to her.

* * *

Large crowds came to look upon the body. Everyone wanted
something that had touched the earthly remains of the saint.
Four Sisters were kept busy touching the body with objects
which people had brought for that purpose. So many came,
and from so far away that, although Bernadette had died on
Wednesday, the funeral could not be held until Saturday.

Her casket rested in the Chapel of St. Joseph on the grounds
of the mother house at Nevers. Above the casket was a stone
with this inscription in Latin:

HERE REPOSES
. IN THE PEACE OF THE LORD
BERNADETTE SOUBIROUS
FAVORED AT LOURDES IN 1858
WITH NUMEROUS APPARITIONS OF THE
MOST BLESSED VIRGIN:
IN RELIGION
SISTER MARIE-BERNARD:
DECEASED AT
NEVERS IN THE MOTHER HOUSE OF
THE SISTERS OF CHARITY
APRIL 16TH, 1879
IN THE 36TH YEAR OF HER AGE
AND THE 12TH OF HER RELIGIOUS PROFESSION
"This is my rest forever and ever.
Here will I dwell, for I have chosen it."
REST IN PEACE

The first steps toward her canonization were taken in 1908. On September 22, 1909, her body was exhumed, as is the custom with persons whose canonization is being considered. The rosary in her hands was rusted, the crucifix on her breast was green with rust, but her body showed no signs of corruption.

In 1910, Pope Pius X signed the Introduction to her cause. On August 13, 1913, she was declared Venerable, and on June 14, 1925, her beatification took place.

On August 3, 1925, her body was removed from the vault, placed in a glass reliquary, and carried to the convent chapel. There it remains to this day, and there it can be seen by all visitors.

(The Chapel of St. Joseph in which Bernadette's body had formerly rested was destroyed in the Allied bombardment of German-occupied Nevers on July 16, 1944. The present tomb of Bernadette, however, remained unscathed.)

On December 8, 1933, the Feast of the Immaculate Conception, Pope Pius XI signed the final decree of canonization. Bernadette Soubirous, the poor little peasant girl of Lourdes, was now inscribed in the Church's great roll of saints.

PART III

THE SHRINE'S FIRST YEARS

CHAPTER VI

EARLY MIRACLES

LOUIS BOURRIETTE was a poor stonecutter who lived in Lourdes. While he was at work in one of the marble quarries of the district, his right eye was half crushed by a chip of stone. For twenty years, he suffered blindness in that eye. Medical science could do nothing to restore his vision. Bourriette's condition excited great pity in Lourdes. Since he was no longer able to work at his trade, most of the inhabitants had given him work at some time or other.

Bourriette heard the stories of the visions which were taking place at the grotto. After the Thirteenth Apparition, he asked his daughter to bring him some water from the spring which had just come forth in the grotto. The girl went to the grotto and returned with a basin full of the water.

"Father," said the child, "it is only muddy water."

"That does not matter," he replied.

After making the Sign of the Cross, the poor stonecutter took a little of the water and rubbed the affected eye. Almost immediately he uttered a loud cry. His sight was returning! He continued to pray and to rub his eye with the water. It was not long before he could see perfectly.

Soon after that, Bourriette met Dr. Dozous in the public square and told him that his sight had returned.

"Impossible," said the doctor. "Your organ of sight is injured to such an extent as to render your cure out of the question. The treatment I have prescribed for you is only intended to soothe your pain, but can never restore to you the use of your eye."

"It is not you who have cured me. It is the Blessed Virgin of the Grotto."

The doctor took a pad out of his pocket, wrote something on it and then held his hand over the stonecutter's good eye.

"If you can read this, I will believe you," he said.

Without the slightest hesitation, Bourriette read the words, "Bourriette has an incurable amarosis, and he will never recover."

Dr. Dozous was astounded. "I cannot deny it," he said. "It is a miracle, a true miracle."

The doctor called in Dr. Vergez of Tarbes, and he, too, was forced to acknowledge that the cure could not be explained by natural means.

The news of this wonderful cure spread rapidly through Lourdes and greatly increased the enthusiasm of Bernadette's followers.

The evening of Bourriette's cure, his fellow quarrymen went to Massabielle and laid out a path for visitors. They placed a wooden balustrade in front of the hollow from which the spring gushed forth and then dug a small reservoir in which the water could collect. This reservoir was the forerunner of the *piscines* of today.

Little two-year-old Justin Bouhorts lay dying of consumption in the home of his parents in Lourdes. The child had been ill almost from birth and had never been able to walk. One of the neighbors, Franconnette Gozo, was preparing the shroud for the child's burial and at the same time was trying to console the mother. The boy's eyes had become glazed, his limbs were motionless, and his breathing seemed to have stopped.

"He is dead," said the boy's father.

A great hope suddenly seized the mother.

"He is not dead," she cried, "and the Holy Virgin at the grotto will cure him for me."

She seized the child from his crib, wrapped him in her apron, and ran toward the grotto crying as she ran, "I am going to the Virgin."

At the entrance to the grotto, the mother fell down on the ground. Then, praying as she went, she dragged herself on her knees to the miraculous spring. Making the Sign of the Cross on the baby and on herself, she plunged the child up to his neck in the icy water of the spring.

The people who were praying before the grotto were horrified.

"You will kill the child," they cried. The mother paid no attention to them.

For a quarter of an hour, she held the boy in the icy water. When she drew him out, he was still motionless. She took him home and laid him in his cradle.

"He is breathing!" she exclaimed.

All night long, she watched him anxiously. The breathing continued and seemed to grow stronger. The next day when the boy awoke, his eyes sparkled with life. He smiled at his mother. He wished to leave his cradle, but his mother would not let him.

On the second day after the visit to the grotto, the mother looked into the room and saw that the cradle was empty. Little Justin, who had never walked in his life, had climbed out of the cradle and was running about the room!

The above cure took place March 4, 1858, the day of the Fifteenth Apparition. This was several weeks before the Lady of Massabielle had revealed her identity.

Many other cures took place at the grotto. The following two are simply examples of many. These occurred in the period between March 5 and March 25, the three weeks during which no Apparitions took place.

Benarte Cazeaux had been confined to her bed for three

years. She had a slow fever and pains in her side. The doctors had pronounced her incurable and had stopped visiting her. She heard about the appearances of "the Lady," and so she sent for some water from the grotto. She drank some of it and also used applications of it. Immediately her "incurable" malady disappeared — never to return.

Blaisette Soupenne had been suffering for several years from a chronic affection of her eyes. Tears flowed continually. She had a severe smarting pain in her eyes. Her eyelashes had disappeared, and the two lower lids were covered by a number of fleshy warts. She had tried in vain all remedies offered by the doctors when she turned to the water from the grotto. Upon the first application, she obtained great relief. When she applied the water for the second time, the cure was complete. The tears stopped flowing; the pain ceased; the warts disappeared, and the eyelashes began to grow once more. Never again did she suffer from this affliction.

The following two cures are reported by Henri Lasserre, one of the first historians of Lourdes. There is a connection between the two, but the persons concerned lived in different towns and did not know each other.

Mme. Rizan, a widow who lived in the town of Nay, was at the point of death. In 1832, she had suffered an attack of cholera and had been growing steadily worse ever since. By 1858, her left side had become totally paralyzed. She could not even move in her bed. Those who attended her had to move her from time to time. Her stomach was unable to bear solid food, and often she vomited blood. She had two painful sores, one on her chest and the other on her back. Long contact with the bed had rubbed her side raw in several places.

The widow had two children, a daughter, Lubin, who lived with her, and a son, Romain, who worked in Bordeaux. When it seemed certain that the mother would die, Lubin sent for her brother. He came to receive his mother's blessing and last farewell. He could not remain long, because his business called him back to Bordeaux. When he left his mother, he was sure he would never again see her alive.

Mme. Rizan heard that one of her neighbors was going to Lourdes. She asked that some water from the grotto be brought back to her. The neighbor promised she would do so.

On October 16, the last moments seemed to have arrived for Mme. Rizan. She was continually spitting blood. A livid tint spread over her emaciated countenance. Her eyes became glassy.

"She will die before daybreak," said the doctor.

In the middle of the night, Mme. Rizan called to her daughter and asked her to go to the home of the neighbor and get the Lourdes water. "It is this water which is to cure me. The Blessed Virgin so wills it," she said.

Lubin promised that she would go the first thing in the morning, and as early as possible she did as her mother wished.

When the invalid swallowed a few mouthfuls of the water, she said, "Oh, my daughter, there is life in this water. Bathe my body with it." Lubin moistened a cloth in the water and washed her mother's face.

"I feel myself cured!" cried the mother.

Lubin next bathed her mother's legs. The swelling subsided at once. The stretched and shining skin resumed its natural appearance.

"I am completely cured," exclaimed the woman who had been on the point of death just a few moments before. The cure was instantaneous.

Mme. Rizan now became very hungry and asked for something to eat. Lubin was very doubtful about this, but, at her mother's insistence, she brought some cold meat and wine. Mme. Rizan partook of both of them, the first time in twenty-four years that she had been able to do so. Then she got up and dressed herself. She was completely well.

In Bordeaux, Romain was talking to a friend when a letter

arrived from his home town in the handwriting of the parish priest, the Abbé Dupont.

"My mother has died," said Romain as he gazed sadly at the envelope.

At length, he broke the seal. The first words to greet his eyes were, "Deo Gratias, Alleluia. Rejoice, my dear friend. Your mother is cured. The Blessed Virgin has cured her."

Romain could scarcely believe his eyes. In amazement he read the letter to his friend.

"Give me that letter," said the friend. "The work of God should be known, and Our Lady of Lourdes glorified."

The friend worked for the *Messager Catholique,* and he saw to it that the letter was published a few days later. It was the indirect means by which another cure took place.

In 1843, a little girl was born to the Moreau family of Tartes. The father insisted upon naming the little girl Marie in honor of the Blessed Virgin, despite the fact that Marie Moreau was not a very euphonious name. He dressed the girl in blue and white, the Virgin's colors, for the first three years of her life.

In January, 1858, when the fifteen-year-old Marie was attending school in Bordeaux, her eyes began to bother her. M. Bermont, an eminent oculist, examined her and said, "The sight in one of her eyes is gone, and the other is in a most critical state."

The distraught parents tried everything medical science could advise, but nothing helped the girl's eyesight. Then one day their weekly copy of the *Messager Catholique* arrived, and M. Moreau read the letter of the Abbé Dupont and the account of the miraculous cure of Mme. Rizan of Nay.

"There," said he, "is the gate at which we must knock."

They decided to say a novena to our Lady. They found that a priest of the town fortunately had some water from the grotto.

The novena began on November 8. The father, mother,

Marie, and another daughter, Marthe, all prayed before a statue of the Blessed Virgin. When Marie went to bed that night, she soaked a linen bandage in the water and tied it about her eyes. She did this mainly to please her father, because he was so anxious for her to do it. She herself had little faith in either the novena or the water.

The next morning when Marie removed the bandage, she uttered a loud exclamation.

"Marthe! Marthe!" she cried to her sister. "I am cured!"

Shortly after that, Marie and her father and mother went to Lourdes to offer thanksgiving to our Lady. Marie resumed her colors of blue and white and wore them till the day she was married. On that day, she presented a blue and white dress to Bernadette. This was the only gift that Bernadette ever accepted, and she wore it for many years — until it could be worn no longer.

The oculist, M. Bermont, was amazed by the cure and signed a declaration to that effect. "A cure which was complete and is still complete. As to the instantaneous nature of this cure, as it has been produced, it is, a fact, beyond comparison, which altogether exceeds the limits of medical knowledge. In which belief I have attached my signature. — Bermont."

All six of the miracles reported in this chapter took place within one year of the time Bernadette first beheld the Blessed Virgin at the grotto of Massabielle. All six were accepted as authentic miracles by the Episcopal Commission which was set up to investigate the happenings at Lourdes. They are just six of the hundreds of remarkable cures which took place during those first few months. There are many such cures still taking place to this day.

Chapter VII

THE BISHOP SPEAKS

FOR almost six months after the First Apparition, the Church stood aloof from the proceedings at Massabielle. The people were flocking to the grotto by the thousands and fervently paying their devotion to the Lady. The local officials were deploring the "superstitious demonstrations" and were trying in every way to prevent people from going to the grotto.

Both sides appealed to the Church.

"We are being persecuted," said the people. "The Blessed Virgin wants us to come to the grotto, and the officials are trying to stop us. Why don't you help us?"

"The people are making fools of themselves," said the officials. "Why don't you tell them that the entire thing is a farce? By remaining silent, you are making things more difficult for us."

But the Church held to a course of stony silence. Abbé Peyramale, Dean of Lourdes, had instructed all the priests under his jurisdiction to stay away from the grotto, and Bishop Laurence of Tarbes upheld him in this. Even after Abbé Peyramale was convinced that Bernadette was telling the truth, the Bishop insisted on a "hands off" attitude.

This was the only wise course to follow, but feelings on both sides were inflamed, and the Bishop's prudence was not appreciated by either side. The Church could not put its stamp of approval on Bernadette's story until it had been proved beyond the possibility of a doubt. On the other hand, it could not say that her story was impossible, for Catholics

63

believe that the supernatural can intervene in human affairs at any time.

On July 28, while the fence was still standing around the grotto, Bishop Laurence took action. The action committed the Church to nothing but an investigation of what had been going on at Lourdes. The Commission which the Bishop established was to ascertain:

"1. Whether any cures have been effected by the use of the water of the grotto of Lourdes, either drunk or used externally, and if these cures can be explained naturally or must be attributed to a supernatural cause.

"2. Whether the visions which the child Bernadette Soubirous professes to have had in the grotto are genuine, and if so whether they can be explained naturally or whether they have a supernatural character.

"3. Whether the object seen in the visions has made any requests or revealed any desire to the child. Whether the child has been told to communicate them. If so, to whom, and what are the requests or desires revealed?

"4. Whether the spring now flowing in the grotto existed before the visions which Bernadette Soubirous claims to have seen."

The Commission worked diligently for many months. Bernadette was called before it and told her story over and over. She accompanied the members to the grotto and pointed out where everything had taken place. Persons said to have been cured by the water were examined and questioned. Physicians, oculists, chemists, psychiatrists, geologists were consulted. Not a stone was left unturned in order to get at the truth. Every fact was checked and rechecked many times over.

Of the hundreds of cures which were claimed to have been effected up to that time, thirty were selected for the closest scrutiny. Six of these, the Commission decided, could possibly have had a natural explanation. Then, in nine of the cases there was very strong evidence of the supernatural, but the

One of the souvenir shops of Lourdes

Statue of the Sacred Heart erected on the grotto grounds by the Diocese of Autun

A street in Lourdes

The sick gathered before the grotto

— Wide World Photos

A fine view of the churches and ramps. The piscines are the three small buildings at the right, against the foundation of the churches

proof was not quite conclusive. The Commission was interested only in cases which left no room for doubt, so these cases were discarded. This left fifteen cures which the Commission at last declared were undeniably supernatural in character. Medical men admitted that these cases were incurable. Yet they were cured, and the cure had been perfect. The evidence was clear and complete. The six cases described in Chapter VI were included among the fifteen that the Commission accepted.

Even though his Commission had found cures that were undeniably supernatural in character, the Bishop still did not speak. He waited three more years to be sure that the cures were not temporary. At the end of this time, the Commission again investigated the fifteen cases and found that there were no signs of a return of the old maladies.

On January 18, 1862, the Bishop spoke. It was indeed, he said, the Blessed Virgin who had appeared to Bernadette.

"Our conviction has been formed on the testimony of Bernadette, and more especially so after taking into consideration the facts which have been produced, and which admit of no explanation but that of Divine intervention.

"The testimony of Bernadette — in itself of considerable importance — acquires altogether new strength — we might say its complement — from the marvelous occurrences which have taken place since the first event. If a tree should be judged by its fruits, we may affirm that the apparition, as narrated by the girl, is supernatural and divine, for it has produced supernatural and divine effects."

The Bishop closed his formal proclamation with a paragraph commending the patience and prudence of the faithful during the trying period when the civil authorities had closed the grotto. He announced that he had acquired title to the grotto and to the adjacent property and that a church would be built there in accordance with the Blessed Virgin's instructions. In order to build the church, he would need the assistance of the faithful in all countries.

The people were elated by this announcement. They had believed all along that the Blessed Virgin had appeared at the grotto. They had considered it an insult to the Queen of Heaven when the grotto had been boarded up. Their sorrow had been great when they had been forbidden to visit Massabielle. Now, the Lady in her quiet, unpretentious way had triumphed. She was to have the chapel and the processions she had requested.

By the thousands, the people flocked to Lourdes to offer their humble prayers of thanksgiving.

Chapter VIII

THE GROWTH OF THE SHRINE

BISHOP LAURENCE had asked the assistance of the faithful in building a church at Lourdes, and the faithful responded with great generosity. From the time of the first apparition, pious pilgrims had been depositing coins at the grotto. As the number of pilgrims increased, the coins increased also, and these were sufficient to defray the expenses of the vast changes that had to be made at the grotto.

Lourdes has been self-supporting from the start. The grounds and buildings are maintained, and salaries are paid entirely from the contributions of the pilgrims. The Diocese publishes no budget, but the usual estimate of pilgrims' contributions runs around $1,000,000. This amount could easily be spent on the maintenance and expansion of the domain of the grotto.

The work of transforming the wild, inaccessible grotto into a shrine worthy of the Virgin began almost as soon as the Bishop had issued his pronouncement. The first church was started, a vast crypt built into the rock of Massabielle. The great rugged slope of the hill was smoothed and cultivated. A broad path was made from the church to the grotto. An iron railing was built in front of the grotto, and a golden lamp was suspended from the roof. Four massive bronze basins were set up to catch the water from the miraculous spring, in order that the people could help themselves to it. A fifth basin, sheltered by a wooden building, afforded the sick an opportunity to bathe in the water. The mill stream, across which Bernadette and her companions had waded, was turned aside. The Gave was thrust back many feet to make room for the esplanade in front of the grotto.

All this work was directed by Abbé Peyramale. He was on the spot almost every minute and spurred the workmen on to ever greater efforts, as if the loss of but a single moment would be an insult to our Lady.

The sculptor Fabisch was brought from Lyons to design a statue of the Virgin which was to stand in the niche where Bernadette had so often seen the Queen of Heaven. It was to represent her as she said, "I am the Immaculate Conception." The sculptor consulted Bernadette constantly and asked her again and again to describe the appearance of the Virgin. Fabisch did the best he could, but when Bernadette beheld the completed statue she said it was not her Lady.

"They are as different as heaven is from earth," she said.

The statue went into the niche nevertheless. No sculptor, no matter how gifted, could portray the supernatural beauty of the Virgin.

April 4, 1864, was a great day in the history of the grotto. It was the day Fabisch's statue of the Blessed Mother was placed in the niche. It was also the day the Church solemnly took possession of the grotto. The Bishop's proclamation had been issued two years before, but the Church had not yet taken possession by any public ceremony.

The weather was magnificent on that day. Lourdes was decked out in flowers, banners, garlands. Bells pealed from the parish church and the other churches of the neighborhood. A procession of 60,000 persons marched from the parish church to the grotto. Sixty thousand persons! And the normal population of Lourdes at that time was five thousand! Bringing up the rear of the procession was Bishop Bertrand Sévère Laurence, accompanied by four hundred priests.

Two persons were missing from the ceremonies. Abbé Peyramale was ill in the hospital, unable even to catch a glimpse of the procession he had so longed to see. Then the most important person of all was missing. Bernadette, too, had taken sick and was unable to attend the ceremonies.

In 1864, before the Crypt was completed, the first pilgrimage from the outside world came to Lourdes. It came from Loubajoc, a small town in the same diocese as Lourdes. This was the beginning of a movement which grew steadily year by year.

Two years later, May 21, 1866, the Crypt was opened to the public. This was the first church to be built at Massabielle. It was the answer to the Lady's request for a chapel. An immense multitude attended the Pontifical High Mass celebrated at an altar erected in front of the grotto.

This time Bernadette was present; she was among the Children of Mary. She had hoped that no one would notice her, but this was not to be. As soon as the ceremonies were over, the crowd surged around her crying, "The saint! The saint!" The nuns of the Hospice had to form a bodyguard around her to save her from being crushed.

In June, 1867, the railway to Lourdes was completed. This railroad was to transform the little mountain town into an enormous pilgrimage center. The number of pilgrims in 1868 was twice that of 1867. During July, August, and September of 1868, more than fifty Masses a day were celebrated in the Crypt.

The Crypt was no more than completed when another church began rising above it, the Basilica with its great tower pointing toward heaven. The Basilica was completed in 1870, but its consecration was delayed by the disastrous Franco-Prussian War.

Those were sad days for France. Her mightiest armies were defeated on the field of battle. Paris was besieged and forced to surrender. By the peace terms France lost the provinces of Alsace and Lorraine, had to pay an indemnity of one billion dollars, and to submit to the occupation of its capital by German troops for three years.

The revolutionary government which succeeded the Empire of Napoleon III was antireligious and tried in various ways to stop the pilgrimages to Lourdes. The faithful became incensed at this persecution and went to the shrine in greater numbers than before. A delegation of 50,000 pilgrims from all parts of France went to Lourdes in October, 1872, to beg the Virgin for courage to bear the woes of their nation. Two hundred and fifty-two banners, each from a different section of the country, were deposited in the new Basilica. As the Bishop accepted the banners of the lost provinces of Alsace and Lorraine, tears filled thousands of eyes, and many sobbed audibly.

The great delegation in October, 1872, was the forerunner of the French National Pilgrimage which is now held for five days every August. This is by far the largest of the pilgrimages; it now includes 100,000 persons every year.

The Basilica was consecrated in 1876. One cardinal, thirty-five bishops, three thousand priests, and a hundred thousand faithful were present at these historic ceremonies. By this time, Bernadette had been in the convent for a number of years. She was to die three years later.

In 1883, the twenty-fifth anniversary of the apparitions, the cornerstone of the Church of the Rosary was laid. This church, which is below the other two, was solemnly opened six years later and was consecrated in 1901 with impressive ceremonies. This completed the trio of churches which today greets the pilgrims to Lourdes.

Pope Leo XIII authorized a special office and a Mass in commemoration of the appearance of the Blessed Virgin to Bernadette. In 1907, Pope Pius X extended the observance of this feast to the entire Church. It is observed on February 11.

In 1912, the name of Lourdes was added to the title of the episcopal see. It is now the diocese of Tarbes and Lourdes. A residence for the bishop was built near the triple churches, and here he resides in Lourdes during most of the pilgrim season. In October, when winter is settling over the Pyrenees, he moves back to Tarbes.

Except for a few minor changes, that completed the development of the shrine as we know it today.

PART IV

OUR LADY VERSUS "SCIENCE"

CHAPTER IX

THE SPIRIT OF THE TIMES

WHY did the Blessed Mother choose to appear to a French peasant girl in 1858?

That is a question which no person can answer with certainty. One can study the facts, however, and see some of the good that was accomplished by the apparitions.

In order to form an idea of the world into which the Virgin appeared, it will help if you will imagine yourself as living in the France of 1858. You will have to imagine yourself in a slightly unfavorable light at first, in order to serve the purpose of the illustration.

You, being a well-educated person, have been living in an atmosphere in which any great dependence upon the supernatural is considered old fashioned. "This is the age of science," you have heard again and again. "We have no need for God in the modern world."

You consider yourself a religious person and do not go along with many of your friends and neighbors who call themselves freethinkers and who say flatly, "There is no God." No, you believe in God. You go to church every Sunday and perform the external duties of your religion.

You are, however, greatly impressed by the strides science has made. You think man can do almost anything. You think of God when you are in church, but you think He has very little place in everyday life. If asked about miracles, you would probably say, "I believe that Christ worked miracles when He was on earth, but miracles don't happen today. After all, this is the nineteenth century."

Almost without realizing it, you have been affected by the spirit of the times. You have not gone as far as your friends who are freethinkers, but you have taken on many of their ideas. If you continue in this attitude, what will happen to you? In religion, as in everything else, there is no standing still. A person goes forward, or he goes backward.

From Lourdes comes a story of a fourteen-year-old girl who says that a Lady has appeared to her in a niche in a rock. You read the story in your local paper, and you feel sorry for the poor deranged child. The alleged visions continue. The peasants and townspeople of Lourdes believe the girl's story even though they cannot see the Lady themselves. You wonder how so many people can be taken in by such a fanciful tale. But, you reflect, these people are ignorant peasants and do not have the advantage of your education. They do not have the "scientific attitude."

Stories begin circulating of sick persons who have been made well by bathing in a spring which the girl claimed had been pointed out by the vision. "Purely imagination," you say. "They only thought they were sick, and so they were cured by autosuggestion."

In your neighborhood is a boy who was stricken several years ago by a spinal disease and has not walked since. The doctors have done everything possible for him but have given up. "He will never walk again," they say. You know the boy well. You stop in now and then to take him little gifts to try to cheer him.

One day you hear that the boy is going to make a trip to Lourdes. You are horrified. "The trip will kill him," you say. "He shouldn't be allowed to go." The doctors agree with you. But the boy insists that he wishes to go, and his parents consent to it.

The trip does not kill the boy. You are at the station when he returns from Lourdes. Instead of being carried off the train on a stretcher, he steps off with the other passengers and walks down the platform.

"It is a miracle!" exclaim the joyous parents.

"Our Lady of Lourdes was very kind to me," says the boy.

You see the boy with your own eyes. He is walking. There is no doubt about it. And he could not walk before.

The doctors who have been taking care of the boy are eminent medical men, but they have said many times that no cure was possible. You question them now. They are puzzled. "The boy is cured," they say. "That is beyond doubt. We are not prepared to say what caused the cure."

The doctors are men of science, and they are imbued with the scientific attitude. They will not admit a miracle, because science says that miracles are impossible. But the boy is cured, and they had said he was an incurable case.

Being a very honest person and a religious one fundamentally, you bow to the facts.

"It is a miracle," you say. "And after all why shouldn't a miracle be worked in the nineteenth century? God is still in His heaven. He made the laws that govern the universe. If He wishes, He can set them aside. God has favored this generation and this country by sending His Blessed Mother to Lourdes. I am going to Lourdes as soon as possible and pay my respects to her."

Isn't it very possible that our Lady appeared in 1858 for the benefit of persons such as you are imagining yourself to be? Unconsciously you had begun to make science a god, and you had exalted man far above his rightful place in the scheme of things. There were thousands like you in 1858. The peasants, as a whole, had not yet been contaminated by this idea. But isn't it likely that they would have been in time? Ideas of this kind filter down from the top.

The boy who was cured of spinal disease suddenly brought you to a realization of how far you had drifted from the simple faith of your forefathers. Similar events were taking place all over France. The faith of thousands in the upper classes was suddenly strengthened, and the faith of the peasants was even more strongly fortified. The so-called scientific spirit was not wiped out by the apparitions — it persists strongly even to this day — but its growth was certainly checked.

By this time, you have become firmly convinced that the Virgin appeared at Massabielle and that miracles have been taking place there. But what of your freethinking friends? You meet one of them and ask him for his opinion.

"What do you think of the boy who was cured at Lourdes?" you ask him.

"I am not prepared to say. I do not know for sure that he was cured. I have not seen him."

"But he lives right down the street. You can walk down right now and talk with him."

"I am not that interested."

"But you are always saying that miracles are impossible. I should think that you would be interested in investigating a reported miracle if for no other reason than to expose it."

"Miracles *are* impossible. Investigation would not convince me."

"But everyone knows that this boy couldn't walk before. He is walking now."

"It could be autosuggestion."

"Autosuggestion can sometimes help cure a nervous disease. Even its most enthusiastic advocates wouldn't claim that it could instantaneously cure a diseased spine."

"The water at the spring might have had something to do with it."

"That water has been tested by chemists and is no different from the other springs in the Pyrenees."

"You keep assuming that that boy was cured. How do I know he was really an invalid?"

"You have seen him many times in his wheel chair."

"Perhaps it was all an elaborate hoax staged by the priests."

"But the priests themselves have not acknowledged the visions at Lourdes to be real. Besides, you have the testimony of the doctors regarding the boy."

"How do I know I can believe the doctors?"

"Do you think that they and the boy and the boy's family would deliberately fake a disease for a number of years? Be reasonable. The boy's doctors, you know, are not religious men. What would they have to gain by such a course?"

"I don't know. All I know is that miracles are impossible."

You leave with the firm impression that no one is less scientific than those possessing the "scientific attitude," that no one is less free to think than is a freethinker.

Chapter X

THE "SCIENTIFIC ATTITUDE"

THE preceding chapter could be criticized on the grounds that it is quite devoid of facts in a book that is supposed to be factual. A person who does not believe in miracles might point out that the cure in that chapter was purely imaginary and proves nothing. Another person, who does believe in miracles, might still wish some facts to back up the sentiments expressed in that chapter. Was the "scientific attitude" really so widespread? Were supposedly religious persons affected by it? Were freethinkers really so averse to facing the facts?

The question of the existence of miracles has already been dealt with in part. As we have seen, the Commission appointed by Bishop Laurence reported fifteen miracles that had taken place in the first few months after the apparitions. These were not figments of anyone's imagination. The chapter following this one will explain how cures are investigated in the most scientific and painstaking manner in order to make sure that the Blessed Virgin does not get credit for cures which might possibly be explained in a natural manner. Later chapters will relate the histories of some notable cures.

The purpose of this chapter will be to give the facts concerning the "scientific attitude" and the opposition to the supernatural which prevailed in the nineteenth century.

The unfortunate truth is that the "scientific attitude" was very prevalent in 1858, and that it persists to this day. Men of "science" have either ridiculed or ignored Lourdes from the beginning. The facts are there to be investigated, but the "scientific" world ignores them.

Cauchy, the great mathematician who died in 1857, boasted of living in a remarkable era "when man has measured the heavens and sounded the depths. . . .The sovereign majesty of God has tumbled; the scalpel of the savant has dissected and reduced that idea to nothing; only the material exists. . . . Reason alone can and has the right to explain everything. The supernatural order is impossible. Religion and faith are superfluous; they are burdens which encumber the human spirit. . . . Science is the modern laboratory of humanity. It alone reigns victorious; it alone emancipates man, releases him from chains, permits him to reach his full height and to search all horizons."

Auguste Compte, the father of Positivism, also died in 1857. Positivism is a philosophy which reduces everything to sense experience and rejects the idea of a personal God. Charles Darwin's book *The Origin of the Species* appeared in 1859. In this book, Darwin explained the origin of man as a process of natural selection and survival of the fittest. This idea could easily lead to a denial of the existence of God, and indeed many of Darwin's followers were atheists. Darwin himself believed in God at the time his book appeared, but he later became an agnostic.

Victor Hugo was in exile in 1858 and was busy writing his antireligious literature. Herbert Spencer was working on the prospectus of his "Synthetic Philosophy." Thomas H. Huxley and John Tyndall were studying at the feet of Darwin.

All such philosophies led to the same inevitable conclusion. Science is all important; there is no need of God.

There was a wave of anticlericalism all over Europe. The anticlericals were strong in France in the Empire of Napoleon III, and later, in the Third Republic, they were to control the government. In Italy, there was a revolt against the temporal authority of the Pope. By 1860, all of the Pope's territory except the city of Rome had been taken from him. That was to go ten years later. When the temporal power of the Pope was taken away, the "liberals" openly boasted that they had destroyed the Papacy.

The latter half of the nineteenth century was a time, in short, when religion was everywhere on the defensive. Materialism was on the march. It paraded under different banners — liberalism, republicanism, radicalism, science, anticlericalism — but all amounted to the same thing. Man had exalted himself to a place where he thought he did not need God. If he did not need God, neither did he need priests, bishops, nor the Pope. There is no telling where the movement might have ended if it had not been checked.

Remember the soldier who cried out during one of the apparitions, "And to think that such follies can take place in the nineteenth century?" This showed the "scientific attitude" was by no means confined to men of science. It had reached the middle classes. And remember the reaction of the peasants who murmured against the soldier? The peasants, at least in the region around Lourdes, were still strong in their faith.

The four officials who played the biggest part in closing the grotto at the time of Bernadette's visions were the Imperial Prosecutor, the Mayor, the Police Commissioner, and the Prefect. Yet these men considered themselves to be religious. They went to Mass every Sunday and always made their Easter duties. It was simply inconceivable to them that any event of a supernatural nature could take place in Lourdes in the nineteenth century.

J. B. Estrade did not believe in the visions even after he had heard Jacomet question Bernadette.

"The commissioner," he says, "suspected in the case of Bernadette a pious fraud; I saw in it only the illusive seductions of a brilliant hallucination. For both of us, the supernatural was out of the question. Could there be any supernatural revelation in such an enlightened century as ours?"

Estrade, as we know, later became completely convinced

that Bernadette's visions were truly supernatural. Dr. Dozous, who had gone to Massabielle in order to "expose" the girl, was an honest man, and so he believed what he could not deny. These men were sincere enough to do some investigating. Most of those who did not believe Bernadette's story did not take the trouble to go to Massabielle. "Miracles are impossible," they said, and that was that. Instead of investigating the miracles which were really true, the unbelievers invented false ones. In March, 1858, the newspaper *Ere Imperiale* said:

"Do not be astonished if there are still to be found persons who persist in maintaining that the young girl is endowed with supernatural power. Consider the ridiculous things they claim:

"1. That a dove hovered the day before yesterday over the head of the child during the time her state of ecstasy lasted.

"2. That the young girl has breathed on the eyes of a little blind child and restored her sight.

"3. That she has cured another child whose arm was paralyzed.

"4. Lastly, that a peasant from the valley of Campan, having declared that he was not the dupe of these scenes of hallucinations, the little girl had the same evening caused his fish to be turned into snakes, which snakes devoured this irreverential man, leaving no trace of his bones.

"Such is the present state of things, and all this might have been prevented at Lourdes if the parents of the girl had followed the advice of the medical men and sent her to the hospital."

By this time, a number of real miracles had taken place at Lourdes, but the paper made no reference to them. Nor did it give any names in the fabricated miracles. Needless to say, the medical men had not advised that Bernadette be sent to a hospital.

When Bishop Laurence announced that he was appointing a commission to investigate the happenings at Lourdes, the exponents of the scientific attitude should have been delighted. This was exactly what they were always advocating, thorough scientific investigation. But they were not delighted. They denounced the action as an insult to reason. The prelate, they said, should be prosecuted in the Court of Appeal and declared unworthy of the functions he exercised. Only two newspapers in Paris defended the Bishop's action.

"If anyone assured me," wrote the editor of *La Presse*, "that a supernatural event, even one most striking, was taking place at this very moment next door to my office on the Place de la Concorde, I would not turn aside to see it."

Thomas Henry Huxley, a disciple of Darwin, was one of the greatest advocates of the "scientific attitude" and was widely acclaimed as an apostle of truth. In 1873, while on a holiday in France, Huxley picked up a book about the history of the miracles at Lourdes. The incident is related by his friend, Sir Joseph Hooker, who accompanied him on the trip.

"He entered with enthusiasm into the subject, getting together all the treatises upon it, favorable or the reverse, that were accessible, and I need hardly add, soon arrived at the conclusion, that the so-called miracles were in part illusions and for the rest delusions. . . . It was the case of two peasant children sent in the hottest month of the year into a hot valley to collect sticks for firewood washed up by a stream, when one of them after stooping down opposite a heat-reverberating rock, was, in rising, attacked with a transient vertigo, under which she saw a figure in white against the rock. This bare fact being reported to the curé of the village, all the rest followed."

Our Lady appeared to Bernadette on February 11, and Huxley, the great scientist, called it the hottest month of the year! To have admitted Lourdes would have been to admit that the ideas with which he had associated his entire life were false. Huxley could not do this. So far as is known, he never gave Lourdes another thought. Practically all antireligious scientists do not deny Lourdes; they do what is worse — they ignore it.

No one was more familiar with the "scientific attitude" toward Lourdes than was the late famous Dr. Alexis Carrel. Along about the turn of the century, Carrel was a student in the College of Medicine at the University of Lyons, France. One day he was called to the bedside of a little girl afflicted with a tubercular abscess in the right hip. Just as many others had done before him, Dr. Carrel tried everything he knew to help the girl, but he had no success. He was ready to give up. The girl's family asked if they might take her to Lourdes. He consented.

One day as Carrel was sitting at a table with a group of instructors and fellow students, someone asked him how he was getting along with his young patient.

"Oh, I sent her off to Lourdes," said Carrel.

Loud laughter greeted this remark. "To Lourdes. And do you think you are going to cure her that way?"

"Well, to tell the truth," said Carrel, "when I permitted her to be taken there, I felt just as you do. I wasn't looking for a cure. Something had to be done, and we had tried everything else. I saw no harm in letting her go to Lourdes. But, gentlemen, I want you to know that this morning I saw my young patient again, just returned from Lourdes. Furthermore, I am happy to be able to give you this amazing bit of news. I found my little patient entirely cured."

Cold silence greeted this statement. Then someone said, "Cured?"

"Yes, completely cured. There is not the slightest trace of the abscess nor of any infection whatsoever. In other words, gentlemen, where for months I met only failure, Lourdes has succeeded in only a few days. And that, I must confess, falls under the category of the miraculous."

This was too much for the "scientific" University of Lyons. One of the professors said, "With such notions as you seem to be entertaining, I believe it is my duty to tell you, Dr.

Carrel, we have no place for you here. The University of Lyons will never open its doors to one with your ideas."

"Very well," replied Carrel, "if that is the case, I shall leave. There are other places that will accept me."

So he came to the United States where great fame was awaiting him as a member of the Rockefeller Institute for Medical Research.

The doctors of the University could very easily have investigated the case of the little girl to determine whether Dr. Carrel were telling the truth. Those with the "scientific attitude," however, are apparently not interested in the truth. They are interested only in denying the existence of the supernatural.

Chapter XI

THE MEDICAL BUREAU

THE Medical Bureau is Lourdes' answer to a skeptical world.

"Everything must be tested by science," said the intellectuals of the nineteenth century.

"Very well then," said Lourdes. "The cures which take place here will be carefully scrutinized in the most scientific manner. We have nothing to fear from science. Science is truth, and we welcome the truth."

In 1882 the *Bureau des Constatations Medicales* was established. English-speaking people usually refer to it simply as the Medical Bureau. The Bureau has a prefect appointed by the Bishop of Tarbes and Lourdes and is open to any doctor who cares to come and visit it. The visiting doctors are free to examine any patients who come to the office, and they are invited to go through all the files. About a thousand doctors a year avail themselves of this privilege. There are usually fifteen or twenty of them there at any one time. They are of all nationalities and of all religious persuasions; many of them have no religion at all.

The purpose of the Bureau is not to treat patients. It was founded solely to investigate patients who claim to have been cured.

The office of the Bureau is in a little building beneath the arches of one of the ramps which extend from the Rosary Church. It is surrounded by iron bars which help protect it from the crowd which surges around it every time a cured patient is taken to the office. A marble statue of St. Luke, patron of physicians, stands on top of the building.

There are two rooms. The first has a large table in the center. Around it are chairs. A bench runs along one side of the room. On the walls are pictures of a few of those who have been miraculously cured at Lourdes. Opposite the entrance door are windows looking out upon the broad walk along the Gave, on the grotto side of the ramp. There is a crucifix, a statue of Our Lady of Lourdes, cupboards containing files and registers, and that is about all. It is in this room that the doctors question the persons who claim to have been cured. It was in this room that Zola sat when La Grivotte came in crying, "I am cured!"

To the left of this first room is a door leading to the other and smaller room. It is here that the doctors make their medical examinations. This, too, is very simply furnished.

As soon as a patient claims to have been cured, he comes immediately to the office of the Medical Bureau. There he is examined, X-rayed, studied. He is asked countless questions about the nature of his infirmity. The record and history of his case from his local doctor is minutely studied.

The Medical Bureau can make four possible decisions regarding the case: (1) The patient is hysterical, and no cure has taken place. (2) The cure is not complete, but an "interesting" amelioration has taken place. (3) A cure has taken place, but some natural explanation might be possible. (4) The cure is complete, and no natural explanation can be given. It is only in the latter cases that the Bureau has any further interest. In these cases, the person cured must present himself to the Bureau a year later in order to ascertain whether the cure has been permanent. No relapses are certified.

Of the one million persons who visit Lourdes each year, about 1 per cent, or 10,000, suffer physical ailments. Of these, about 150 are known to have been favored by a cure of some kind every year. About 10 or 15 of these 150 are certified by the Medical Bureau as having been cured in a manner that cannot be explained by science.

Many cures which have been worked through the intercession of Our Lady of Lourdes are never recorded at the Medical Bureau. Hundreds of persons have been turned away without their names having been taken because their ills were due to nervous or other conditions which could possibly have been cured in a natural manner. Others who are cured never go to the Bureau at all, and therefore the doctors have no way of knowing about them. Numerous cures take place many miles from Lourdes; many sick persons have Lourdes water brought to them by friends. These people cannot be examined by the doctors, hence their names do not go into the files. Many cures which seem to be genuine are rejected because the patient has brought no certificate from his local doctor, or because the certificate is too vague. This certificate is all important; it is the only means of assuring the doctors at the Bureau that the cured patient was really suffering from any malady.

Many doctors seem to fear being trapped into admitting a miracle and send such vague documents as this one: "I, the undersigned, Doctor in Medicine, Mayor of my Commune, hereby certify that Madame X is suffering from a disease the nature of which my philosophical and political opinions forbid me to specify."

The lady who brought this certificate was cured, but her cure could not be registered.

An English doctor sent this certificate: "Jane Smith is suffering from skin trouble." Naturally, it was of no use.

In all fairness, it must be admitted that many doctors send excellent certificates and are ready to admit that they cannot explain the cure of their patients by natural means.

The number of miracles is not important anyway. The remarkable thing is that *any* miracles take place. Miracles are not the reason for the existence of Lourdes. It is certain that the Blessed Virgin did not wish a shrine established there just so she could heal bodily ailments. The chief value of miracles is that they establish the supernatural character of the shrine, and one miracle could do that as well as a hundred.

The word *miracle,* incidentally, is never used by the Medical Bureau. It merely reports that the cures cannot be explained in any manner known to science. The power to certify miracles belongs to the ecclesiastical authorities.

The ordinary layman usually refers to the cures as miracles. There is nothing wrong in this so long as he remembers that the Church is the sole judge in such matters.

There is just one fact that might prevent these cures from being miracles. The Medical Bureau says that the cures cannot be explained by any means known to science. But isn't it possible that there are remedies not yet known to science? Could it be, as the study of medicine makes further advances, that these cures may be found to have had a natural cause after all?

This argument is a familiar one. It is the last refuge of those who refuse to believe.

We have already traced, in part, the attitude of those who are determined not to believe. At first, they ignored the cures. When that was no longer possible, they ascribed the cures to autosuggestion. But the most ardent supporters of autosuggestion have never claimed that it would instantaneously restore destroyed tissue. Nor would autosuggestion work in the case of a baby, and many babies have been cured. All cures of nervous diseases are rejected by the Bureau, because they might be attributed to autosuggestion.

Some said the cures were due to the curative properties of the water, but the chemical analysis of the water disproved this. Some said they were due to the shock of the cold water. If so, why should the patients have to come all the way to Lourdes? Cold water can be found almost anywhere in the world. Besides, by no means all of the cures take place in the baths. Many take place at the Blessing of the Sick in Rosary Square; some take place in the hospitals; others take place on the return trip from Lourdes.

With all other arguments gone, the skeptics can always fall back upon the fact that there are probably a number of physical laws that have not as yet been discovered. Does this argument have any validity? Very little, it would seem. Science will no doubt make many great discoveries in the years and centuries to come, and it will do much to alleviate human suffering. But does anyone believe that science will ever be able to create instantaneously more than an inch of bone? This is what happened in the case of Pierre de Rudder whose case will be more completely discussed in a later chapter. Such a thing violates that part of the Law of Conservation of Matter which says that in nature nothing is ever created. This is a fundamental law of science.

Or consider the case of Madame Biré who came to Lourdes in August, 1908, with her right eye stone blind and the sight of her left eye almost gone. She could barely distinguish light from darkness with her left eye. Her optic nerves were atrophied, and she had been pronounced incurable. She was not able to bathe in the *piscines* on the morning of her arrival because of the immense crowds. She was taken to the grotto, and there she lay saying her rosary. At the end of the last Mass, the Blessed Sacrament was taken back to the Rosary Church. As It passed Madame Biré, she cried out and then fainted. When she came to, she saw the crowd that had gathered about her, and she knew she had been cured.

An eminent oculist happened to be at the Medical Bureau. He examined Madame Biré and declared that the atrophy remained as before. According to all laws of science, he said, she was still blind. Yet she could read the smallest type in the newspaper.

Madame Biré was rather worried about this cure. It seemed too much to expect that God would go on working a continuous miracle for her. Within a few months, however, she was relieved of her worry, because her eyes and nerves were gradually restored to normal.

No one can believe that some as yet undiscovered law of science will enable a person to see without the use of his optic nerve!

Is it possible that the local doctors who send the certificates fake the reports and certify disease which never existed in order that miracles might be claimed? The possibility was mentioned in an article about Lourdes which appeared in *Fortune* in 1934. *Fortune,* which is certainly not a religious magazine, immediately dismissed the possibility with the statement that it is difficult for the skeptic of skeptics to believe that *all* local doctors have been charlatans.

What of the doctors at the Medical Bureau? Are they inclined to be rather lenient, to give the Blessed Virgin the benefit of the doubt in most cases?

Just the opposite is true. Persons who have sat in on the examinations are unanimous in declaring that the head of the Bureau and his associates try in every way possible to find a natural explanation for every cure. They could not be more exacting in their examinations if they were the most convinced atheists. Doctors who have come to the Bureau ready to criticize have left admitting that everything is handled very fairly and very thoroughly. Some are reticent about expressing an opinion concerning the cures, but most admit that they cannot explain them. Many have said that only the intervention of the miraculous can explain the healings.

This is the Medical Bureau that is open to all men of science but which has so largely been ignored by them. There is nothing secretive about it. It is there for all to investigate. It is Lourdes' challenge to the "scientific attitude." It is her challenge to those who say that there is no such thing as a miracle and no such thing as the supernatural.

To all who hold such beliefs, Lourdes says, "Come, gentlemen, and see for yourselves. Our doors are always open to you."

CHAPTER XII

APPROACHING THE GROTTO

THERE was no railway through Lourdes in 1858, but with so many pilgrims flocking to the city, it was soon necessary to build one. Today, Lourdes can be approached from Bordeaux by way of Pau or from Paris by way of Tarbes.

The pilgrim coming by way of Pau catches a glimpse of the shrine before he gets into the station. The tracks run along the bank of the Gave for some distance. Across the river, the grotto can be seen with many pilgrims kneeling before it. In the niche is the statue of our Lady. Rising above and behind the grotto is the Basilica with its tapering spire.

Most pilgrims come from the more populous regions of northern France. Lourdes is a long day's ride from Paris. A person traveling third class can make the round trip for fifteen dollars. He can stay for five days at one of the two hundred or so inexpensive hotels or pensions, eat at the less expensive restaurants, and make the entire trip for about twenty-five dollars. Even if one can afford more luxury, third class is the preferred way to travel to Lourdes. The person who travels to Lourdes first class is not a pilgrim — he is a tourist.

If one arrives at the Lourdes station in the summer, the season of pilgrimages, he will probably see a number of persons either arriving or leaving. The station is a busy place at this time of the year. On the platform, he will probably see a row of wheel chairs waiting to take the sick from the station to the hospital. Beside each wheel chair stands a *brancardier*, or stretcher bearer, one of the noble volunteers in the service of the sick.

The first sight of Lourdes, the town, is disappointing. The buildings are dingy and depressing looking. Even the better hotels are garish, in their brightly colored stucco. Shepherds drive their flocks through the narrow streets. Slow-moving ox-carts block the way. Dogs, cats, chickens, and geese get under the feet of pedestrians. Automobile horns blow raucously, clearing a way through the confused traffic. Streetcars clang up and down the streets. There are hundreds of tawdry souvenir shops selling cheap rosaries, crucifixes, statues, and musical plaques which play the Lourdes Hymn, and some of the proprietors are not above hawking their wares from the doorways like side-show barkers.

The visitor is probably disappointed. So this is what he came so many miles to see, a commercialized tourist center!

A big open truck comes by, and because the streets are narrow, the visitor is forced back against a souvenir shop. Already keenly disappointed by what he has seen, he is now greatly annoyed. He looks to see what has caused him this inconvenience. Laid across the truck, side by side, are many stretchers containing sick pilgrims. It is too hot for blankets, and the visitor sees bodies without legs, legs swollen to the size of the body, legs that are shriveled almost to nothing. He sees bodies that are deformed in all sorts of horrible ways. Great, wide, unseeing eyes stare out at him; other eyes are closed. There are faces that are twisted, faces that are covered by repulsive sores, faces that are scarcely recognizable as faces.

"God forgive me for feeling as I did," murmurs the visitor.

Suddenly Lourdes has taken on a new meaning. These suffering pilgrims who have come to implore the intercession of the Blessed Mother — they are the spirit of Lourdes, not the ugly looking buildings, not the squalid souvenir shops.

Yet, how could things be any different? With pilgrims flocking to Lourdes by the thousands, accommodations had to be built for them, and they could not afford — nor would they wish — to live in luxurious hotels. Most of the pilgrims wish to take home souvenirs, and since many of them could not afford the more expensive items, something within the range of their meager pocketbooks must be furnished. A rosary is a rosary whether it is made of cheap glass or of the best mother of pearl, and just as acceptable to our Lady. Cheap as they may be, the souvenirs are all of a religious nature. In this, Lourdes differs from the ordinary tourist center.

There are two ways by which the grotto may be approached. One is across the Gave by the Old Bridge, the successor to the Old Bridge crossed by Bernadette. This route follows, roughly, the path taken by Bernadette. But how different everything is today! There is a bustling city now where there used to be a lonely countryside. This is the new Lourdes. The old Lourdes centers about the castle on the other side of the river.

The best way to approach the grotto is by the Boulevard de la Grotte and St. Michael's Bridge. To stand by the entrance gate and gaze toward the triple churches is to view one of the most impressive sights in the world. There is a smooth green lawn with neat, trim paths and with white marble statues glittering here and there in the sun. Behind this park is the Esplanade bordered by giant green trees. Last of all there are the triple churches — next to the grotto this is the most famous sight in Lourdes.

Just outside the gate, there is much noise and confusion. Hawkers cry, "Candles! Bouquets for the grotto!" People are talking in all languages. Automobile horns add to the din.

Inside the gate, the atmosphere is completely different. This is sacred ground. There is no commercialism, no confusion. All is quiet. Pilgrims are walking here and there, most of them lost in quiet prayer or meditation.

Two large statues of the Archangels Raphael and Gabriel guard both sides of the gate. A little farther on, the visitor

passes a statue of St. Michael trampling the dragon. At the left
is an impressive group cut out of Carrara marble, the Health
of the Sick. A sick man on a stretcher is supported by a
brancardier and comforted by a nurse, both of whom represent Charity. A priest, representing Faith, is directing the
patient's thoughts to God. The Blessed Virgin, with arms
outstretched, fills the sick man with Hope.

A little farther along the grassy path is the great Breton
Calvary. This statue was given to Lourdes by the chief
dioceses of Brittany. Another group, the Apparition of the
Sacred Heart, was given by the diocese of Autun. At the left
is the Victory monument and chapel dedicated to the Allied
soldiers who died in World War I. Far to the right, near the
river, is the Asile of Our Lady. This is the hospital in which
most of the sick pilgrims stay. Near the Asile are two small
dormitories for members of the women's branch of the Hospitalité, the organization of persons who have volunteered to
care for the sick.

Proceeding along the center path, the visitor next passes
a statue of the kneeling figure of the Curé d'Ars. After that,
he comes to the crowned statue of Our Lady of Lourdes
which is inside a circular iron fence. At night, this statue is
illuminated by electric lights.

The Esplanade, which extends to the churches at the far
end, begins at the statue. It is in this tree-bordered Esplanade
that the Blessing of the Sick takes place every afternoon, rain
or shine.

The churches which stand at the far end of the Esplanade
have been criticized as being architecturally ineffective, and
many have gone so far as to call them ugly. If this is true,
it must be remembered that they were built in a hurry. Our
Lady had requested a chapel, and the authorities carried out
her request with all possible speed.

But most visitors do not consider the churches ugly. The
Church of the Rosary, with its graceful, curved ramps reaching out from each side of the imposing doorway, reminds one

of St. Peter's with its colonnades, and the Esplanade reminds him of the Piazza in front of St. Peter's. This comparison brings to mind the fact that St. Peter's has often been criticized as being architecturally inferior, yet the ordinary visitor always finds it breath-takingly beautiful.

The ramps are huge driveways which reach from the Esplanade to the dome of the church. At regular intervals, on both sides of these drives, are large statues of saints. If one stands in the middle of the Esplanade, or Rosary Square as it is often called, he has a full view of the arches supporting the ramps. The highest ones, of course, are those nearest the church. They become lower as the driveways approach the ground. The highest arches in the right ramp are open. They afford a passageway to the grotto. A beautiful picture is framed by these arches. In the foreground, the river sparkles in the sun. Behind it sheep graze on the rolling green hills, which stretch out in front of the lofty Pyrenees. The sky is a deep rich blue. On the stone bench which runs along the bank of the river sit many pilgrims. Some are saying their rosaries. Others are eating their simple lunches or chatting quietly.

The headquarters of the men's branch of the Hospitalité is under the next arch. It is almost hidden by the dense rows of trees which border the square. Housed in the lower arches is the Medical Bureau. The remaining arches are very low and are used for less important purposes. Two of them serve as storage space for candles. During the summer months, pilgrims leave so many candles at the grotto that they cannot all be lighted at once. The overflow must be stored away and used later. Little carts travel between here and the grotto all the time. A fresh candle is lighted every time one burns down.

Later the three churches will be described but the pilgrim has not as yet reached the heart of Lourdes. The grotto *is* Lourdes, for here is the place the Blessed Virgin hallowed by her presence.

Chapter XIII

THE GROTTO

BEWARE of pickpockets" is the sign that greets the visitor as he passes through the arch on his way from the Rosary Square to the grotto. The warning is displayed in many different languages. It is a sudden shock to see it on this sacred ground, but unfortunately it is only too necessary. Thieves have even been caught dressed as nuns with wax hands folded on their breasts so their own hands would be free for picking pockets.

Beyond the arch, the visitor passes three little buildings which have been built into the rock of Massabielle on the north side. They are in the shadow of the Basilica which rises above them. They are the *piscines,* or baths. It is here that the sick pilgrims, and many who are not sick, immerse themselves in the water of the spring. A crowd of curious spectators is usually waiting outside the *piscines,* for many cures have taken place there.

Next are the taps, or twelve bronze hydrants, where the pilgrims can obtain Lourdes water. A crowd is always gathered about with bottles and other containers. Almost everyone who goes to Lourdes wishes to take some of the water home with him.

The first sight of the grotto itself is likely to be disappointing. The imitation grottoes that one has seen so often are very attractive and have water trickling down over beautiful colored rocks. Surely this black, smoked-up hollow can't be the famous grotto. This is not a fitting place for the Queen of Heaven to set her feet. Yet, wasn't her Divine Son born

in a cave similar to this one — a cave fit only to be a shelter
for beasts?

The three openings in the rock are still there, but their
appearance has been changed somewhat since Bernadette's
time. The miraculous spring is in the lower one, to the left
as the visitor faces the grotto. An altar has been built in this
niche, and an iron fence is in front of it. There are two openings in the fence, one for the entrance and one for the exit
of pilgrims. Rosaries, bouquets, and all kinds of thank offerings are hung on the spikes of this fence. Inside the fence,
hundreds of candles are burning on both sides of the altar.
Strung on wires overhead and stacked thick in the corners
are hundreds of crutches and sticks and surgical stays left by
persons who were cured at the grotto and no longer had
need of them. Numerous as they are, these represent only
a small proportion of the cripples cured at Lourdes. In the
deepest recess of the rock is a wire basket, an improvised
"post office" in which pilgrims drop petitions to our Lady.
When the basket is full, the unopened letters are burned by
one of the chaplains.

In the niche where the Lady appeared stands Fabisch's
statue, which represents the Virgin as she said, "I am the
Immaculate Conception." A halo of silver letters around her
head has this statement in French, *"Je suis l'Immaculee Conception."* At her feet in gilt letters are the words she actually
spoke, *"Qúe soy l'Immaculado Councepciou."* The Virgin
always spoke in the patois of the district, the only language
Bernadette understood at that time.

The statue has a gleaming white robe and a sash of deep
blue. There are golden roses on her bare feet, and a glittering
rosary of fifteen decades hangs from her right arm. Her hands
are clasped in prayer across her breast. It is an attractive
statue according to mortal standards, even though Bernadette
failed to see in it anything like the heavenly beauty that
she had beheld.

Beside the statue is a rosebush. The eglantine which

originally stood there was long ago carried away by souvenir hunters. The present bush was planted in 1912. Soil from Nazareth was mixed with soil from the grotto and packed about the roots.

An open air pulpit stands outside the rock to the right. Here priests who are the leaders of various pilgrimages exhort their followers to prayer. It would be interesting to know how many different languages and dialects have been spoken from that pulpit.

Rows of benches stretch from the grotto halfway back to the river, over the filled-in land where the Gave flowed in Bernadette's time. During the summer months, there is usually a crowd of people on this smaller Esplanade in front of the grotto. Some pray quietly on the benches. Others kneel in front of the grotto saying their beads. Some pray with their arms outstretched, a favorite method of praying at Lourdes. A number file through the grotto leaving their candles as they go. Many kneel and kiss the ground as they approach the grotto. Everyone who visits Lourdes is impressed by the great amount of prayer. The very air seems to be charged with prayer.

The hundreds of candles burning within the grotto are a fascinating sight. There are long candles, short candles, thin candles, thick candles. There are inexpensive candles which burn quickly and go out with a sputter; there are candles made of the finest beeswax which burn slowly and steadily. Each candle represents someone's prayer — a prayer of thanksgiving, a prayer of petition, a prayer of veneration. They burn day and night, summer and winter. The walls of the grotto are black from their smoke, and the air near by is warm from their flames.

J. K. Huysmans, the brilliant French writer, was enthralled by the candles: "What wild rendings of heart and what trembling hopes they reveal! How many infirmities, sicknesses, domestic distresses, desperate supplications, conversions, and maddening terrors do they stand for! This grotto is the shelter

The grotto

— From *I Met a Miracle*, courtesy St. Columban's F.M. Society

The procession of the Blessed Sacrament

— From *I Met a Miracle*, courtesy St. Columban's F.M. Society

The sick gathering before the grotto

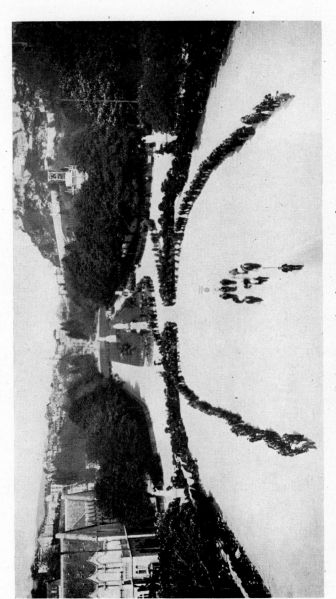

A pilgrimage entering the grotto grounds

The sick waiting to enter the piscines

—Wide World Photos

Pilgrims fill the esplanade before the triple churches

The façade of the Rosary Church. The Basilica towers behind

— Wide World Photos

and refuge of all racked with the anxieties of this world, the refuge to which all the crushed in life fly for protection; it is the last resort of the condemned, and of afflictions that nothing can alleviate; all the suffering of the world is pressed into the narrow space.

"See how the candles weep the tears of mothers in despair, and perchance give an exact counterpart of the sorrows that consume them; some weep hurriedly, pouring down hot tears; others are more restrained, shedding slower drops; and all are faithful to the charge entrusted to them; all, before final extinction, writhe increasingly while their flames shoot up in a last cry to the Virgin!

"Clearly, some are more eloquent than others in pleading with God; and there is no doubt that the humblest are the most persuasive; the pretentious columns of stearin, bought on the spot or sent by the wealthy, because of the pomp they proclaim, have less chance, despite the greater length of their supplication, of favorable acceptance; and certainly the divine pity inclines toward the poor little tapers lighted in bundles, which mingle their yearnings and their lights together, and combine, as they do in church, in one common supplication. They are a true likeness of the poor and destitute who help one another, whilst the aristocratic candles live alone and apart."

Huysmans referred to the man who took care of the candles as our Lady's gardener — "a real gardener in a blue apron with pockets, smooth shaven, with his gardener's tools, pruning knife, rake, shovel, and a wheelbarrow as big as a little cart."

Huysmans did not mention the gardener's name. Perhaps he did not know it. Jean Marie Laffont was guardian of the grotto from its first years until shortly before his death in 1927.

The Laffonts lived in a little village on the outskirts of Lourdes and used to bring corn to the mill run by Bernadette's father. When the father returned the corn as flour, Bernadette often went along.

Jean Marie was present at the Tenth Apparition, February

25, 1858. Bernadette was already looking at the vision when he got there. He could see nothing but a hole in the rock. Being a very small boy, and anxious to get a better view of the scene, he climbed a tree. The branches were entangled with eglantine. His weight shook the branches and rustled the vine. Bernadette called to him, "Come down. Come down. You will offend the Lady." Later, she told him that the Lady only smiled.

When Bernadette and the others left, Jean Marie went up to examine the spot where the vision had stood. When he got there, he trembled so violently and felt so ashamed that he left at once. But then and there he decided that he wished to spend his life in the service of our Lady. He went to work at the grotto shortly after.

Jean Marie was the only one allowed to go up into the niche and trim the eglantine and wash the statue. When asked how he felt all alone up there with the statue he said, "I beg the Virgin to keep me near her and to take me up higher still, for at those moments when I am up there, I no longer love the earth."

Jean Marie died on the Feast of the Epiphany, 1927, at the age of 89.

The task of the guardian of the grotto is not a light one. Thousands of candles are offered during the summer months, and everyone wishes his candle burned at once. As the candles burn down, they have to be collected. The melted wax is put into barrows and taken away. The candles that cannot be lighted during the summer are kept for the winter months. On the coldest days of winter, Jean Marie was always at the grotto — as his successor is now — tending to the candles, although the number of pilgrims had dwindled to a handful.

Besides tending to the candles, the guardian of the grotto must arrange the hundreds of bouquets that are left there, and remove the flowers when they have faded. He must also prepare for the many daily Masses which begin at 5:30 every morning and continue until 9:30.

Only a trickle of water from the miraculous spring comes down the rock. Most of it is piped to the taps where everyone is free to help himself. It gushes forth at the rate of 1000 gallons an hour, so there is plenty for everyone. Some of the water is also piped to the baths. An immense reservoir of it is kept under the Rosary Church. This reservoir is filled during the winter and at other times when there are not so many pilgrims. Thus, an adequate supply of the water is assured for the season when thousands of pilgrims draw upon it.

After a visit to the grotto, the visitor now goes back through the arch under the ramp to have a look at the three churches.

Chapter XIV

THE TRIPLE CHURCHES

THE lowest and the newest of the three churches at Massabielle is the Rosary. It is built in the Byzantine style and has a magnificent Romanesque doorway which faces Rosary Square.

Huysmans, who constantly complains of the ugliness of Lourdes, says the interior of the church looks like a roundhouse. "Only the rails and the central turn table are wanting, instead of the high altar, to enable the engineers to come out of the side-wings and perform their evolutions on the broad walks of the Esplanade."

It is true that the church is built in the form of a rotunda, but the comparison with a roundhouse seems a little unkind. Another writer, Aileen Mary Clegg, compares the church with a beehive. "The domed roof, the crowds incessantly entering it and leaving it, the unending murmur of the rosaries and of subdued conversations, enforce the idea." This is a kinder comparison, and one with which the pilgrim would be much more inclined to agree.

The huge central dome covers the sanctuary and part of the nave. A semicircular transept extends from each side of the circle thus formed, and a semicircular apse extends behind it. The shape of the church resembles a three leaf clover with a thick stem or, a better comparison would be, the ace of clubs. The transepts and the apse are each divided into five chapels, one for each mystery of the rosary. Each of these chapels has a large mosaic picture over it. The church is richly decorated. All lighting is from the central dome which is more than fifty feet high.

Besides being the lowest and the newest of the three churches, the Rosary is also the largest, and it is used at all ceremonies attended by big crowds. There is very little ventilation in this great church, which is at times crowded with several thousand persons, but the French and other continental people are not as concerned by this fact as Americans would be.

There are four ways of reaching the Crypt, the church that is in between the other two. One can walk up either of the two ramps which ascend from Rosary Square, or he can climb either of the two flights of steps at the sides of the great door of the Rosary Church. Whichever way he chooses, he finds himself on one of the two driveways which meet behind the dome of the Rosary Church. Stretching out behind the dome is a flat space which leads to the entrance to the Crypt. The Crypt is cut out of the rock of Massabielle. This is the oldest of the three churches and is the only one that Bernadette saw. The church is entered by way of a long corridor, the walls of which are lined with many plaques, thanksgiving offerings for favors granted at Lourdes.

The Crypt is short and very low. In the center is an altar around which twenty-three small lamps are kept constantly burning. Many other altars are set in recesses in the walls. Above each altar is a deep slanting window. Gold mosaics decorate the walls. There is always a priest in the sacristy of this church to hear confessions. Usually a group of people are standing near the entrance of the sacristy waiting to go to confession.

Above the Crypt is the Basilica with its tall tapering tower reaching toward heaven. There are four bells in this tower, and every half hour the carillon plays the first line of the famous Lourdes' hymn. The richness of the interior is striking. Gilded railings enclose a white marble altar surmounted by a white statue of Our Lady of Lourdes. Above hang sanctuary lamps of gold and silver. A gilt inscription in very large letters of the Virgin's words to Bernadette encircles the entire church.

From the roof of the nave hang banners from practically every country of the world. There are twenty-three stained glass windows, all of which represent episodes in the story of Bernadette. The massive pulpit is made of Canadian oak.

Mementos line the walls of the church. What stories could be told about them! There are swords, guns, plumes, paintings, bridal wreaths, First Communion ribbons, plaques, and all sorts of other votive offerings. Each has been placed there in thanksgiving for some favor received. Here are stories of narrow escapes on the battlefield, stories of wrecks at sea, stories of quiet sacrifice, stories of crippled children suddenly made well. In the sacristy is a magnificent monstrance of solid gold. It is four and a half feet high and contains more than a thousand diamonds, fifteen emeralds, dozens of rubies and other precious stones. Pictures of Mary and the Holy Eucharist are carved into the gold. It is a superb piece of workmanship.

The Way of the Cross has been erected on the hill to the left of the Basilica. Each station is represented by a group of lifesize statues. A stairway has been built on the side of the mountain, and many pilgrims ascend from station to station on their knees. "Penitence! Penitence!" the Lady had said, and these pilgrims are carrying out her injunction.

The Fourteenth Station is at the very summit of the hill. Having completed this station, the pilgrim pauses to view his surroundings. The Esplanade, with its border of green trees, stretches out below him. In front of that is the park whose neat, symmetrical little paths look as if they had been laid upon a great green carpet. Just outside the park is the newer section of the town, and across the river is picturesque old Lourdes clustered about its ancient castle, which stands on the top of another hill. Forming a giant backdrop for the town and the castle are the lofty Pyrenees whose snow-capped peaks are outlined against the azure sky. To the south, the Gave glistens in the sunlight as it emerges from the mountains that have cradled it. It follows its silent course through the town, turns, and then flows by the smaller esplanade in front of the grotto. After that it loses itself among the green hills upon whose slopes sheep are contentedly grazing. All is serene and quiet. The Blessed Mother could not have chosen a more beautiful spot for her shrine.

Chapter XV

THE SICK AND THEIR CARE

"AT LOURDES it is a joy to flout the microbe," says an English nurse. "We find our Lady putting microbes and bacilli firmly in their place."

In the Asile, or hospital, patients are segregated according to sex but not according to disease. Persons with many different kinds of sicknesses, including tuberculosis in its most advanced stages, are packed together in one room as close as the beds will fit. The rooms are poorly ventilated, and the air is germ ridden. No persons with contagious diseases are admitted, but there are innumerable chances for infection.* Anywhere else on earth disease would sweep through the hospital like wild fire. But there has never been a case of a sick person's contracting a disease at Lourdes. This flouting of the microbe, this suspension of the usual laws of nature, is the perpetual miracle of Lourdes. It is a miracle that has been going on for almost ninety years.

A pilgrimage from somewhere arrives in Lourdes almost every day during the summer months, and every pilgrim train has its share of the sick. They are met at the station by the *brancardiers*, placed on trucks and taken directly to the Asile. This is not a hospital in the usual sense of the word. No medical treatments are given; no operations are performed. The Asile is merely a place for the patient to sleep and eat

---

* Contagious diseases are those carried by germs in the air. Infectious diseases are those transmitted by contact with the diseased or with substances carrying the germs. Scarlet fever is an example of a contagious disease. Tuberculosis is an example of an infectious disease,

between his trips to the grotto, the baths, and Rosary Square. It is unlike other hospitals, too, in that the patient is not questioned regarding his financial status. The crippled son of a poor chimney sweep is as welcome as a millionaire and is given the same treatment.

It is possible to see more suffering in one summer day in Lourdes than it is in a modern city in ten years. Modern society deems suffering to be a public disgrace and keeps it hidden. In Lourdes suffering is not regarded as a disgrace. The sick are not hidden away as if they had done something of which they should be ashamed. They are carried through the streets in open ambulances, laid out in large public rooms in the hospitals, carried to the grotto where all may see them.

The sight of these unfortunate creatures is not always pleasing to the healthy pilgrims, but if they are real pilgrims they have not come to Lourdes for a pleasure trip. They have come to pray and to do penance. The sight of the sick usually moves them to prayers of compassion. "Lord, save our sick," is heard over and over. The pilgrims are also reminded to say prayers of thanksgiving for their own good health, that priceless gift which God could have withheld from them had He so chosen.

The sick at Lourdes are constantly attended by an organization called the *Hospitalité de Notre Dame de Lourdes*. This organization consists of volunteers who serve without pay. They make it possible for thousands of sick persons to come to Lourdes who would not be able to afford the trip if they had to pay attendants to take care of them. The women in this organization act as nurses, dishwashers, waitresses, and cooks. They work under the direction of the Sisters who are in charge of the hospital. The men serve as *brancardiers*, or stretcher bearers.

The *Hospitalité* dates back to 1880. In August of that year, the Viscount de Roussy de Sales saw that an invalid was having some difficulty getting off the train, and he offered to help her. As he pulled her little wheeled stretcher box through the city, he called upon two of his friends to help him. This was the beginning of the organization which now numbers about 700 members. There is another organization, the *Hospitalité de Notre Dame de Salut* which has about a thousand members and serves only during the time of the National French Pilgrimage.

The women of the *Hospitalité* wear distinguishing headdress and medals. The special badge of the *brancardiers* are the shoulder straps called *bretelles*. When the *brancardiers* actually carried stretchers, these straps served a very practical purpose; the ends supported the poles of the stretchers. Today, they are used principally as a means of identification, for there is very little actual stretcher work. New *brancardiers* wear straps of webbing; those with ten years of service to their credit wear leather ones. The stretcher bearers may dress as they please, but they invariably wear the tight blue beret of the Pyrenees.

Many members of the *Hospitalité* serve all summer. Others, especially the men, who cannot afford to leave their work for such a long time, serve for shorter periods. Many persons devote their vacations every year to this self-imposed task. Some of the volunteers have been cured at Lourdes and serve in this way to express their gratitude. The organization is extremely democratic. Members of royalty, bankers, merchants, tradespeople, workingmen serve side by side; gladly they perform any menial task that comes their way. A rich young American used to leave his yacht at Monte Carlo every year while he served as a *brancardier*.

Each stretcher bearer is given a small handbook containing the rules he must follow. He "must be ready to bear cold and heat, sun and rain, hunger and thirst, and long waits." He must not exceed a walking pace when in charge of invalid chairs. He must not smoke when in charge of sick persons. He must know how to carry the sick so that they suffer the least possible jolting.

Brancardiers gather at the hospital every morning between

6:30 and 7:00. At a signal from the Sister in charge, each takes a wheel chair, goes to a bed, wraps a blanket around the patient, and lifts him or her into the chair. The long procession of wheel chairs starts toward the grotto for the Mass of the Sick. The *brancardier* takes his rosary out of his pocket and takes the lead in praying the five Sorrowful Mysteries. The patient makes the responses. Often the *brancardier* and the patient are praying in different languages, but that makes no difference. At Lourdes the common bond of devotion to the Virgin transcends the barriers of language.

The stretcher bearers park the chairs in long rows in front of the grotto, and then they return to the hospital to bring more patients. At 7:30 the Mass starts under the beautiful blue southern sky. The sick occupy the space nearest the altar and are fenced in by the *brancardiers* standing behind them. The other pilgrims are behind the stretcher bearers. During the Mass, a priest comes down among the invalid chairs and distributes Communion to the sick. Communion goes on continuously every morning, sometimes for as long as three hours.

When the patients have had time to make their thanksgiving after Communion, the *brancardiers* wheel them back to the hospital for their breakfast. The rosary is said again on the return trip. The sick have their breakfast in the open air. Leaving all spiritual considerations out of the matter just for the moment, this stay in Lourdes must be a very pleasant experience for the patients who are well enough to enjoy it. Many of them have come from slum districts. What a treat it must be for them to be here in the fresh air, bathed by the warm friendly sun, surrounded by the lofty peaks of the Pyrenees!

After breakfast, the patients are wheeled to the baths. Then they go back to the hospital for lunch. In the afternoon, they go to Rosary Square for the Blessing of the Sick. By the time the patients are taken back to the hospital after this blessing, both they and the *brancardiers* have put in a long day. The latter are usually ready to go back to their hotels for a rest before their evening meal.

Pushing the wheel chair is not the only work of the *brancardiers*. They must do everything they are told. In his book *Tramping to Lourdes,* John Gibbons tells us that he was once told to wipe a boy's face and keep on wiping it. "Why I remember it is because he had not got a face, only a hideous sore of running filth."

The *brancardiers* must pray all the time, no matter what task they are performing. John Gibbons also tells the following incident: "They sent me once to fill some bottles with the Lourdes water, and even that is not quite so easy as it sounds. The taps run very slowly, and one takes one's turn in an endless queue to get to one. They are placed very low down near the ground, so that one has to stoop nearly double to fill one's bottle. . . . I had six bottles, and every time I came back with an empty one, I had to take my place all over again in the queue. The arrangements, I was thinking, were bad. Could they not have raised the level of those taps? But, of course, they could. For the matter of that, they could have laid the water on by pipe to every hotel in Lourdes. Or there must be enough money in the world to carry it through to Paris or London if it works by a sort of automatic miracle cure for the lazy. Only it does not. And just then one of the head *brancardier* people came up to me. I was not doing it properly at all. I ought, of course, to have been praying all the time."

Our Lady must smile when she watches the work of the Hospitalité. These people are carrying out her injunction to do penance, and they are making it possible for many sick to go to Lourdes who would otherwise not be able to go.

Our Lord must be pleased too, for He said, "As long as you did it for one of these, the least of My brethren, you did it for Me."

Chapter XVI

THE BATHS

LOUIS BOURRIETTE, the blind stonecutter of Lourdes, was the first person to discover the miraculous properties of the spring in the grotto. The water was in great demand after he was cured of his blindness. Many people were not content merely to drink the water or to use it as a lotion. They wished to bathe in it. A wooden building was erected for this purpose, but it soon proved to be too small to accommodate the ever increasing crowds. The present *piscines* were built in 1891.

The *piscines* are three low brick buildings near the grotto. Each building contains three baths. One building is for men; five of the six baths in the other two buildings are for women and the sixth one is for children. That is about the proportion of each among the pilgrims. Almost twice as many women as men visit Lourdes; this probably accounts for the fact that there are more women cured than men.

There is a railing about the buildings, and in the space between the railing and the *piscines* the sick await their turn to be admitted. Outside the railing there is usually a large crowd.

Everyone prays: the pilgrims outside the railing, the patients inside, the *brancardiers* who bring the patients and who wait to take them back, the attendants inside the buildings.

"Lord, save our sick!" the cry goes up from several hundred throats.

Then there is a thunder of Aves followed by "Mary, we love thee!"

The praying never stops. The faithful are massed for a veritable assault upon heaven.

There are no doors in the buildings. Curtains serve both as doors and as partitions. The curtains are white with blue borders and are embroidered with our Lady's monogram. Each of the nine sections is divided into two parts. One is used as a dressing room; the other is the bath.

Three attendants help the patient to undress to his undergarments. Then he goes behind the curtain to the other section. Here three more attendants assist him. One helps him remove the rest of his clothing, the other two wrap him in a sheet which is still wet from being used by the preceding pilgrim. If the patient is able to walk, he descends the three steps into the water. If he is not able to get into the water by himself, he is lowered into it by the attendants. There is a space wide enough on each side of the bath for an attendant to stand.

The pilgrim makes a fervent act of contrition, and if he is able to walk, he goes through the water to the end of the bath where he kisses a statue of the Blessed Virgin. Then he sits down in the water and is laid on his back. Some pilgrims submerge completely, others keep their heads out of the water. The water is not deep, just deep enough for one to submerge if he lies on his back.

All this time, the patient and the attendants are praying. There is a card just below the statue of the Virgin which contains the prayers to be said while the bathing is going on: "Blessed be the Holy and Immaculate Conception of the Blessed Mary, Mother of God! Our Lady of Lourdes, pray for us! Mother, have mercy on us! Our Lady of Lourdes, heal us for the greater glory of the Holy Trinity! Our Lady of Lourdes, heal us for the conversion of sinners! Health of the sick, pray for us! Help of the suffering, pray for us! O Mary, conceived without sin, pray for us who have recourse to thee!"

The bath takes but a very few moments. The attendants

work with such quiet efficiency that hundreds of persons are able to bathe within a few hours' time.

The water in the baths is changed only twice a day. Patients with running sores, with cancerous growths, and with every kind of infectious disease are plunged in one after another. Yet, as in the case of the hospital, no case of infection has ever resulted. Not every patient who bathes in the *piscines* is cured, but none ever gets any worse.

Some years ago, certain French doctors tried to have the baths closed on the grounds that they were unsanitary. Dr. Vincent, a member of the French Academy of Medicine, sprang to their defense as did a great number of other doctors. The document containing the proofs used in the defense of the baths, and signed by three thousand medical men, is on file in the library of the Medical Bureau.

The *piscines* are small, dark, and poorly furnished. The water is discolored from the diseased bodies that have plunged into it. Yet it is here, as Huysmans says, "that the Virgin, turned into a bath attendant, works; it is in this damp den, and with this putrid water, that she operates.

"And you are seized with distress; you almost tremble, withdrawing suddenly within yourself, when you reflect that she keeps unseen in this narrow room, that you are perhaps brushing against her, and that in a moment, if she will, she may prove her presence by a cure."

Often she does prove her presence by a cure. Bertha Radford Sutton, a member of the Hospitalité, describes an incident of which she was a witness. A woman who seemed more dead than alive was borne in on a stretcher. Miss Sutton and her two fellow workers started to undress her. The agony of being undressed was so great that she fainted. When she came to, she insisted upon being lowered into the water, and her wishes were acceded to. As she was taken out of the water and put back on the stretcher, she fainted again. She was carried into the outer compartment. Suddenly, to the amazement of Miss Sutton and the others, her eyes opened and she sat up. Color came back into her face; her eyes were full of new life. She felt her feet and her legs and then she began to whisper, "But, *mon Dieu*, what has happened? There is no more pain. I can move, bend, twist."

The nurses dressed her carefully, but Miss Sutton purposely pulled her stocking fairly energetically. There was an awed, amazed whisper, "No pain. *Can* it be true?"

The woman had no shoes, so the nurses put a blanket on the damp floor, moved some chairs, and let her get off the stretcher. There was no ecstasy, relates Miss Sutton, "only a whole new view of heaven and earth in her eyes as she rose and walked." She couldn't believe her good fortune. "Why, *mon Dieu*, there is no pain," she murmured over and over. "No pain, anywhere."

At moments like that the Blessed Virgin seems very close indeed.

The woman's husband, an unbeliever, had promised to "consider the question" if she were cured. "We joined our prayers with hers," says Miss Sutton.

Only a very few of the afflicted are cured in such a sudden manner. Some are cured on their way home or after they have returned home. The majority of pilgrims are not cured at all. The bath, however, is never taken in vain. Some favor is always granted. That is why many perfectly healthy pilgrims bathe in the water of the spring. The uncured patient becomes more resigned to his suffering. All pilgrims are strengthened in their faith. And that is more important than the cure of any physical ailment.

Chapter XVII

THE BLESSING OF THE SICK

THE Blessing of the Sick is a sight never to be forgotten. This blessing takes place in Rosary Square nearly every afternoon during the pilgrim season. Even bad weather does not always interfere with it. Sometimes it is held in a downpour of rain. At such times, those in the procession and the onlookers, many of them helpless invalids, are drenched to the skin. Yet the ceremonies go on as if the sun were shining benignly, and no one seems to notice the rain. One would expect many cases of pneumonia to result, or at least a few head colds, but this never seems to happen.

Occasionally, if the weather is bad and only a few pilgrims are in Lourdes at the time, the Blessing of the Sick is held in the hospital. This, however, is unusual; the blessing in the Square is the rule.

The baths are closed at four o'clock every afternoon. At that time, the pilgrims begin gathering in front of Rosary Church. They form a border around three sides of the Square. The open side is the flight of steps leading up to the Church. A gap is left in the end opposite the steps so the Procession of the Blessed Sacrament can enter the Square. In the front are the stretcher cases, and behind them are the patients in wheel chairs. Next are the patients who are able to walk. Benches have been provided for them. Behind the sick are the *brancardiers* who brought them, and last of all are the pilgrims who are well.

At the time of the National French Pilgrimage, this human

wall about the Square is eleven or twelve persons deep. The sick alone may number as many as twelve hundred. The other pilgrims fill every available space from which the procession can be viewed. The ramps, the terrace above Rosary Church, the hill which has the stations of the Cross — all are covered by the great throng.

The patience displayed by the sick is amazing. Sometimes the sun beats down mercilessly. At other times, they are soaked by a sudden mountain storm. Those on the stretchers are often unable to brush away the flies that crawl over their faces. But not a word of complaint escapes their lips. The Blessed Virgin seems to endow them with special strength while they are in Lourdes.

So many sick gathered in one place! The sight is enough to melt the heart of the most hardened. It impresses one more here on the Square than it does in the hospital. It seems as if all the sick in the world have been brought together.

The most heart-rending cases are those of the sick babies. They are so small, so helpless, to be enduring such agony. And the mothers of these children! Oh, if only something could be done for them! But something can be done for them. Other pilgrims can pray, and pray, and pray.

While the crowd waits on the Square, the Blessed Sacrament is brought to the grotto, and the procession is formed. First come the Children of Mary in their white veils, then men with lighted candles, then monks in their habits, and next priests in their cassocks and surplices. Acolytes with torches and incense precede the Bishop who carries the Blessed Sacrament. He walks beneath a large canopy. Sometimes there are so many persons in the procession that an hour elapses between the time the Children of Mary leave the grotto and the time that the Blessed Sacrament arrives on the Square.

The people in the Square say their rosaries aloud while they wait. They are led by priests in their own tongue. Then from the direction of the grotto comes the sound of singing. The procession has started. Under the archways of the ramp it is possible to get an imperfect view of the procession as it starts on its way. Everyone in it is singing.

Suddenly a voice is heard in the middle of Rosary Square. A priest stands there with arms outstretched. He is praying, and the crowd echoes his words after him. The priest prays in the language of the majority of the pilgrims present. Usually it is French, but when pilgrimages from other countries are present it can be in any number of languages. Occasionally it is English.

"Jesus, Son of David, have pity on us!" cries the priest.

"Jesus, Son of David, have pity on us!" the multitude roars the words after him.

"Master, save us, we perish!" implores the priest.

"Master, save us, we perish!" Again the crowd takes up the cry.

The procession moves closer. It makes its way along the edge of the river, past the Asile, past the gateway leading to the city, past the War Memorial, past the Crowned Virgin. The children of Mary reach the opening in the crowd. They proceed across the Square and take their places on the steps of the Church. The rest of the procession follows. The singing continues. Many of the men are carrying banners which catch the rays of the afternoon sun. The sky, which is the roof for this vast outdoor church, has appropriately the colors of the Virgin in it; puffs of fleecy white clouds float upon a background of deep rich blue.

The Blessed Sacrament enters the Square. The singing stops, but the prayers of the priest and the people continue. The canopy which has been held over the Bishop is replaced by a gold umbrella. The Bishop, holding the Sacred Host in a glittering gold monstrance, turns to the left and begins the Blessing of the Sick. He is accompanied by a number of priests in vestments and by acolytes swinging censers.

Opposite each sufferer, the Bishop stops for a moment and moves the monstrance in the form of a cross. Slowly he walks past the line of patients stopping at each one. The healthy pilgrims drop to their knees as the Sacred Host passes.

A tense expectancy hangs over the crowd. Sometimes a sick person has suddenly gotten up and walked as he was blessed. Will something of the kind happen today? The crowd prays with ever increased fervor.

In the middle of the Square, the priest is still calling out to heaven, "Lord, he whom Thou lovest is sick!"

The crowd echoes the wail which was raised by Martha and Mary when their brother Lazarus died. Jesus took compassion on Martha and Mary and raised their brother to life. Will he heed the prayers of the crowd today and restore some sick person to health?

The Blessed Sacrament moves on.

Red, swollen eyes look up imploringly at the Host; crippled arms are raised in supplication, then slowly lowered.

The prayers of the priest go on, and each one is repeated by the throng.

"Lord, that I may see!

"Lord, that I may hear!

"Lord, that I may walk!

"Lord, say but the word and Thy servant will be healed."

The Host reaches the front steps of the Church. Then traversing the length of the Square, the Bishop starts coming up the other side. The Blessing of the Sick is half over, and still there have been no cures.

"Lord, if Thou wilt, Thou can make me whole," comes the prayer of the priest.

"Thou art Christ, the Son of the Living God."

The Blessed Sacrament moves on. It is approaching the last of the patients. Now the last sick person is being blessed.

No miraculous cures have taken place today.

"Lord, Thy will be done on earth as it is in heaven," says the priest, and the words are solemnly repeated by the crowd, a sign of resignation to the Divine Will.

It is a sight to bring tears to one's eyes — all these stricken persons and their friends and relatives beseeching God for a cure. When no cure comes they say, "Lord, Thy will be done." Here one beholds a remarkable sign of faith.

The Bishop mounts the steps. The moment for the general blessing has come. A bell tinkles. The Bishop raises the Host and makes the Sign of the Cross over the people. They murmur prayers of thanksgiving. The doors of the Church slide open, and the Procession moves into the interior.

The Procession of the Blessed Sacrament and the Blessing of the Sick are over. The patients are taken back to the hospital, and the crowd disperses.

Is Lourdes a concentrated effort to obtain a miracle?

A casual observer might be inclined to think so. He sees the sick everywhere he goes. They wait their turns to bathe in the *piscines,* and the healthy pilgrims stand outside praying, "Lord, save our sick." The impression is strengthened by the Blessing of the Sick. The sick are lined up for a special blessing, and the crowd is crying, "Lord, that I may see! Lord, that I may hear! Lord, that I may walk!" It is not to be wondered that the observer comes to the conclusion that Lourdes is a great healing center and that the well have come to pray for the sick.

Such, however, is not the case.

We have already seen that of the one million persons who go to Lourdes each year only 10,000 are suffering physical ailments. This is one per cent of the total. The ninety-nine do not come to pray for the one. The prayers are for all humanity, not for a few who happen to have diseased bodies.

The series of prayers which the pilgrims repeat after the priest before and during the Blessing of the Sick are forty-six in number. The great majority of these are acts of belief and acts of love. Sixteen are addressed to the Mother of God and implore her prayers. Six — and only six — are prayers for cures, and they could be applied to the soul as well as to the body.

It is only natural that the sick will pray to be cured and

that their friends and relatives will join in these prayers, but the curing of bodily ailments is not the principal preoccupation of Lourdes. It is rather the alleviation of the deadlier misery of the soul.

Margaret Gray Blanton in an article entitled, "A Protestant Looks at Lourdes," says, "These cures make Lourdes such a storm center of argument! It is unfortunate that they take so much attention from something just as valuable: a recrudescence of faith and valor, a relighting of the flame of courage which, sick or well, is needed by us all."

It is only natural that the healings receive great attention. It is dramatic when a crippled person suddenly gets up and walks. One such cure receives widespread notice. Ten thousand persons, however, come to Lourdes and have their souls purified and receive no attention at all.

But the cures of the soul are not always undramatic.

A parish priest in a certain part of France had a tremendous amount of work to do when he organized a pilgrimage to Lourdes. It is not surprising, therefore, that one of the tickets fell into the hands of an unbeliever. Etienne, a giant of a man, thought this a huge joke. He decided he would make use of the ticket so that he could see the "superstition" of Lourdes at firsthand.

Etienne accompanied the pilgrimage everywhere it went in Lourdes. While the others walked with their hands folded in prayer, he sauntered along with his hands in his pockets. While the others prayed reverently at the grotto or filled containers at the taps, he leaned nonchalantly against the railing in front of the grotto, gazing in amused contempt at the pilgrims' piety. What stories he would have to tell his freethinker friends when he went back home!

The only reason Etienne's peculiar behavior had escaped the notice of the priest was that the latter had been kept very busy directing the pilgrimage. Everyone else had noticed the man.

While the pilgrimage was organizing to take part in the Procession of the Blessed Sacrament, the priest seized Etienne by the arm.

"My friend, you are the very man I need. We have a new banner, and it is very heavy. You are strong; carry it in the procession."

He thrust the banner into the hands of the surprised Etienne. It was a great floating satin banner with the Crucifix painted on one side and the name of the parish on the other. Before the man could say a word, someone had removed his hat.

Etienne shrugged his shoulders. Well, why not? He had come to Lourdes as a joke; he might as well carry the joke to its conclusion. He marched off carrying the banner; on his face was a cynical smile.

Everyone sang, *"Parce, Domine, parce populo tuo."* Once the priest moved up the line and asked Etienne if the banner were too heavy. Etienne shrugged him off, and the priest went back to his singing.

Later, the priest caught up with him again. The man appeared to be suffering from the heat.

"Let someone else carry the banner for a while," said the priest. Etienne refused roughly. The priest was puzzled. None of his parishioners had ever spoken to him in such a manner. Who was this man?

A short time later, the word was passed down the line that the man carrying the banner seemed to be sick. The priest hurried to him again. The man looked white and agonized. Perspiration and tears poured down his face.

Alarmed, the priest motioned for another man to come forward to take the banner.

"This banner, my friend . . . " he began as he reached to take it from Etienne's grasp.

"Banner!" gasped Etienne. "You call this a banner! It is God on His Cross I have carried, and His sorrows have broken my heart. No, no, I will finish my Way of the Cross, and look you, then, Monsieur le Curé, I will make my submission."

A cure of that kind demonstrates God's mercy more than all the cures of the body and is more typical of the spirit of Lourdes.

CHAPTER XVIII

THE TORCHLIGHT PROCESSION

THE torchlight procession is the final and most colorful of the day's ceremonies at Lourdes. It takes place every summer evening after darkness has descended on the valleys of the Pyrenees.

Every pilgrim who wishes to take part may secure a candle and join the procession. It starts at the grotto and covers the same ground as was covered by the Procession of the Blessed Sacrament in the afternoon. Instead of stopping at the Church of the Rosary, however, it goes up the right ramp, past the entrance of the Crypt, and down the left ramp.

A pilgrim who is in Lourdes for two nights — and most pilgrims are there at least as long as that — would enjoy taking part in the procession one night and watching it the other night. He would certainly wish to take part in it because he has come to Lourdes to pay honor to the Virgin, and this procession is one of the ways of doing so. On the other hand, the sight of the procession, seen from a height overlooking the square, is unforgettable.

Watched from across the river the procession is a scene of almost unearthly beauty. Out of the enveloping blackness shine myriads of lights. The candles burning in the grotto make a great concentration of light. The front of the Basilica is ablaze with electric lights, and on the spire are the huge illuminated letters N D L (Notre Dame de Lourdes). In the park stands the crowned statue of our Lady brightly lighted. While the first part of the procession is coming down the left ramp, the last part is just leaving the grotto. To observers standing across the river, the procession going up the one ramp and down the other looks like a gigantic broken wheel of light.

The marchers sing the famous Lourdes hymn, the Canticle of Bernadette. This hymn has sixty stanzas, and after each stanza comes the refrain:

Ave, Ave, Ave Maria!
Ave, Ave, Ave Maria!

At each *Ave,* every candle is held aloft in a triumphant gesture. The hymn is sung in many different languages, and usually those at the end of the procession are several lines behind those near the head.

The Canticle of Bernadette may be called the theme song of Lourdes. It is sung on the pilgrim trains going to and coming from Lourdes; parts of it are sung at various times throughout the day; and it is *the* hymn of the torchlight procession. It has no great value as music and many of its sixty verses are poorly rhymed, but it has a haunting quality. A person who has once visited Lourdes will have the whole scene flash back before his mind the moment he hears a line of the song. It was written by Gaignet and was published in 1874. The words tell the story of Bernadette and the appearances of the Virgin.

The marching continues for about an hour. At last the people in the procession gather in the square in front of the church and form themselves into a gigantic M. A Bishop on the steps of Rosary Church holds up his hand, and the singing stops instantly. Then he raises his hand again, and the thousands of persons gathered on the square burst forth in the singing of the *Credo.*

Visitors to Lourdes have often said that this singing of the *Credo* is one of the most impressive things they have ever known. A moment before, each of the pilgrims had been singing in his own language, and the result was a confused but not displeasing jumble. Now suddenly, everyone is declaring his belief in God in the Latin, universal language of the

Church. It is as if the intense devotion of the pilgrims and their common purpose has momentarily freed the world from the confusion of tongues.

With the singing of the *Credo*, the ceremonies at Lourdes have come to an end for the day. Some of the people go back to their hotels immediately. Others, before retiring for the night, make one last trip to the grotto to bid good night to Our Lady of Lourdes.

THE CASE OF PIERRE DE RUDDER

THOUSANDS of remarkable cures have taken place at Lourdes since 1858. Some stand out especially because of the dramatic circumstances under which they took place or because of the nature of the malady cured. We shall consider a few of these more interesting cures in this and in succeeding chapters.

The case of Pierre De Rudder is mentioned in almost any discussion of the miracles of Lourdes. Pierre De Rudder was a farm laborer in the employ of the Viscount du Bus de Gisignies who had a castle near Jabbeke, Belgium, about halfway between Bruges and Ostend. Pierre was a model workman and was highly esteemed by his employer. On February 16, 1867, he saw two young woodcutters trying to move the trunk of a large tree which they had just felled not far from the castle. He offered to help them, and they gladly accepted his offer. He took an ax and began to chop off the branches of a bush that was in the way. At the same time, the two young men raised the trunk with levers and tried to push it forward. Suddenly the tree slipped and struck De Rudder with such violence that it threw him to the ground. His left leg was caught under the trunk of the tree and was crushed by the weight of it.

The Viscount du Bus was very much distressed by this accident which had befallen his faithful workman and sent at once for Dr. Affenear of Oudenbourg. Upon examination the doctor found that both bones in the left leg had been broken. He set them and bound the leg in a starched bandage.

De Rudder suffered intensely during the next few weeks and begged to have the bandage removed. When at last this was done, it was found that fresh complications had arisen. The broken ends of the bones were swimming in pus, and, deprived of their periosteum, they had not even begun to knit. In addition to this, a large ulceration had formed on the instep of the foot.

After many months of attending the patient, Dr. Affenear despaired of a cure. There is little wonder that he did, for at that time antiseptic treatments were hardly known. A fragment of dead bone which had become lodged in the tissue had to be removed. Three more doctors were called. They all agreed that the leg should be amputated, but De Rudder would not give his consent. He was confined to his bed for a year, enduring great pain the entire time. When he got up, he had to drag himself along on crutches, for he could not put his bad leg to the ground. He washed his wounds two or three times every day and wrapped the broken limb in linen bandages. This method of treating a fracture complicated by suppuration naturally produced no results.

Since De Rudder was not able to work, his family became very poor. Two years after the accident, Viscount du Bus allowed his former workman an allowance of eight francs a week. Because they were already living rent free in the cottage owned by the Viscount, they were able to eke out an existence on this allowance.

The years went by without bringing any relief. De Rudder was tortured with pain every waking minute. Toward the end of December, 1874, Dr. van Hoestenberghe of Stahille examined the leg. At the inquiry which was held later, he had this to report:

"De Rudder had a wound on the upper part of the leg; at the bottom of this open wound could be seen the two ends of bones about an inch apart. There was not the slightest appearance of cicatrization. Pierre suffered very much and had endured his broken leg for eight years.

"The lower part of the leg could be turned in any direction. The heel could be lifted so as practically to fold the leg in half. The foot could be twisted until the heel was in front and the toes at the back.

"All these movements were limited only by the resistance of the muscular tissues."

Dr. Verriest of Bruges was another of the doctors who had been called in on the case. In the middle of January, 1875, he told Dr. van Hoestenberghe that he could obtain no improvement in the case. He said that the evening before De Rudder had positively refused to go to the hospital at Bruges and have his leg taken off, and that in consequence he was giving up the case. Dr. van Hoestenberghe agreed that this was the only thing to do.

De Rudder had long wished to make a pilgrimage to the shrine of Our Lady of Lourdes at Oostacker, near Ghent. This grotto is modeled after the one at Lourdes. The Viscount, however, would not hear of such a thing. He told De Rudder that he would gladly pay all his doctor bills, but he would not make himself ridiculous by financing a pilgrimage. Didn't De Rudder know that miracles were impossible? But De Rudder did not know this. He did not have the advantage of the Viscount's education.

In July, 1874, the Viscount died, and his son succeeded him to the title and to the possession of the castle. On April 5 of the following year, De Rudder again presented himself at the castle and asked permission to go to Oostacker. The young

Viscount's cousin and fiancée happened to be at the castle that day. "Moved by curiosity," she related, "I wanted to see De Rudder's leg. He took off the linen bandages, which were saturated with pus and blood. The odor was insupportable. The last folds of the bandage were stuck to the wound, and could not be easily detached. At this sight I instinctively recoiled."

The new Viscount willingly permitted De Rudder to undertake the pilgrimage. He did not believe in miracles any more than his father had, but he did not have the heart to refuse the unfortunate man's request. It was decided that De Rudder would leave two days later on April 7.

That evening Marie Wittizacle, a neighbor of the sick man, helped him dress his wound. She, too, saw the broken bones.

On the evening of April 6, M. Edouard van Hooren and his son, Jules, paid a visit to De Rudder. They stayed nearly two hours, chatting about the trip he was to make the following day. Marie Wittizacle was present also. Three weeks later the three signed an attestation in which they affirmed "that they saw, on April 6, 1875, the broken leg of De Rudder; the ends of the fragments of bone were piercing through the skin, and were separated by a wound about three centimeters in length."

During the inquiry Edouard van Hooren was asked:

"Did you sign this certificate?"

"Yes, we signed this certificate."

"Do you know what you signed?"

"Yes, yes, certainly."

"Was it actually the day before the pilgrimage that you saw De Rudder?"

"Yes, the day before, in the evening. I was at his home with my son and Marie Wittizacle."

"What did you see?"

"Pierre uncovered his leg to dress it, and he folded the leg so as to show us the two ends of the broken bone."

"The bones were not united?"

"No; it was just as I had always seen it before — the leg could be turned and twisted in any direction."

Early the next morning the faithful neighbor, Edouard van Hooren, was at De Rudder's house to bid him Godspeed.

Pierre's wife changed the dressing, and she and the daughter saw once more that the leg was still in the same condition. It was four o'clock and still dark as De Rudder and his wife set out for the railroad station. Dragging himself along on his crutches and supported by his wife, it took more than two hours to travel the mile and a half to the station.

He rested while waiting for the train, in the little cottage of Pierre Blomme, the gatekeeper. Blomme testified later that he saw De Rudder's leg swinging back and forth below the knee.

"But what are you going to do at Oostacker with a leg like that?" he asked. "You had much better stay home."

"Others have been cured at Oostacker; why not I?" said De Rudder.

The train arrived in the station. Pierre Blomme, Balthassar de Jaeger, another station employee, Jean Duclos, a shoemaker of Jabbeke, and Pierre's wife lifted the helpless cripple into the train. Jean Duclos and his mother traveled with the De Rudders as far as Bruges. Duclos later gave testimony that he saw that the leg was broken below the knee and that the bandage around the leg was wet with offensive matter.

At Ghent they had to get into an omnibus for the trip to Oostacker. When they arrived the driver, a big burly fellow, lifted Pierre to the ground. As the broken leg swung to and fro, the driver laughed loudly and called to those who were looking on, "Look, here is a man who is losing his leg!" The driver stopped his laughing a moment later, however, when he looked inside the carriage; the floor was soiled with blood and matter. He complained loudly to all who would listen.

De Rudder dragged himself the short distance to the grotto. Although he stopped frequently to rest, he fell exhausted upon one of the benches in front of the little chapel. His wife gave him a drink of water from the fountain. Some of the passing pilgrims accidentally brushed against his leg and caused it to swing back and forth. This caused him intense pain.

At length with a great effort, he rose and went around the grotto twice. He tried to go a third time but was unable to move further. He had to sit down in front of the statue of the Blessed Virgin to rest. He began to pray. First, he asked pardon for his sins. Then he begged Our Lady of Lourdes the grace to be able to earn a livelihood for his wife and children.

Suddenly, he felt a strange sensation. He was upset, shaken, agitated. Forgetting his crutches, without which he had not taken a single step in eight long years, he rose and walked through the rows of pilgrims. He knelt down in front of the statue. Then, astonished to find himself kneeling, he cried, "I am on my knees! O my God!"

He arose and walked three times around the grotto. He needed no help! His wife seeing him cried, "What has happened? What are you doing?" Then, like a bolt, came the realization that her husband was cured. She fainted.

An excited, babbling group of pilgrims crowded around De Rudder, asking him many questions.

Accompanied by his wife and many others, Pierre went to the chateau of Mme. la Marquise Alphonse de Courtebourne. There the leg was examined. The leg and the foot, both of which had been swollen a short time before, had gone down to their normal size and the plaster and the bandages had fallen off as a result. The two wounds were healed and the two broken bones were united in spite of the distance that had separated them. They were firmly fixed together. Outwardly, the two legs were alike in every respect.

After the examination, Pierre went back to the grotto to offer his prayers of thanksgiving to Our Lady of Lourdes.

When he got off the train at Jabbeke that evening, the gatekeeper, Pierre Blomme, stared at him in blank amazement.

When he recovered his powers of speech all he could say was, "You did well not to listen to me!"

As De Rudder walked home, his friends and neighbors saw him and stared as they would at one who had risen from the dead. An eager crowd accompanied him to his house. His fifteen-year-old daughter, Silvie, fell into his arms and sobbed. His three-year-old son, who had never seen Pierre without crutches, scarcely knew his father. Marie Wittizacle and the two Van Hoorens had heard the report of the cure, and they hurried to see with their own eyes what they thought must be impossible.

The Viscount had gone to Brussels with his mother and his fiancée. They were at the table when a wire came announcing the remarkable news. The Viscount was impressed. "I have never believed in miracles," he said, "but if De Rudder is cured, it is really a miracle, and I shall believe."

A few days later, a number of prominent citizens of Jabbeke composed a document. In it they stated that they knew positively that Pierre De Rudder had been declared an incurable cripple and had been considered so by all who knew him, but that he had returned cured from the shrine of Oostacker. Among the signatures attached to this document was that of the Viscount du Bus, the man who had not believed in miracles.

A novena of Thanksgiving was begun in the parish church of Jabbeke. Out of a population of 2000 almost 1500 made the novena.

Dr. Affenear heard the news and hurried to Jabbeke. He examined the leg very carefully and could not overcome his emotion. Great tears rolled down his face.

"You are completely cured, De Rudder," said the doctor. "Your leg is like that of a new-born baby. Human remedies were powerless, but what doctors could not do, the Blessed Virgin has done."

Dr. van Hoestenberghe was a freethinker, and he refused to believe the news. When he came from Stahille to see for himself, he found Pierre hoeing in the garden. The doctor was thunderstruck. In order to prove that he was really cured, Pierre jumped up and down. Upon examining the leg the doctor found a scar below the knee and one on the instep, evidences of the disease which had been cured. He found the inner surface of the tibia quite smooth. There was no lameness whatsoever. The left leg was just as long as the right one.

In 1892, the doctor wrote a letter to the head of the Lourdes Medical Bureau in which he reviewed the facts in the case. This was the year that Zola visited Lourdes, and so Dr. van Hoestenberghe concluded his letter with the words: "Probably this letter will find you with M. Zola. If this be so, I should be glad for him to read it, and, if he would allow me, to say to him these few words: 'Sir, I was an unbeliever as you are; De Rudder's miracle opened my eyes, hitherto closed to the light. I still doubted sometimes, but I studied the Christian religion and prayed. Now, I can affirm, on my honor, that I believe absolutely, and that with belief I have found happiness, and an interior peace, which I had never known before.'"

Zola had left Lourdes before this letter arrived, but it is extremely doubtful that it would have made any impression. His was a closed mind, not willing to see the truth.

What of the driver of the omnibus that had taken De Rudder to Oostacker? He, too, had been a skeptic. When he heard that the cripple whom he had lifted from the omnibus had been completely cured an hour later, his skepticism vanished. He became a Christian and remained so for the rest of his life.

Eighteen years after the cure, Dr. Royer, a Frenchman, undertook to investigate the facts once more. De Rudder and most of the witnesses were still alive at that time. While on the train on the way to Jabbeke, the doctor met M. Taffeniers, a merchant who was on his way to Bruges. In the discussion that followed, it developed that the merchant was a freethinker. At once, the doctor asked him to assist in the investigation, and the merchant accepted. An unbiased report was assured by the fact that one of the parties making the investigation was a Christian and the other a freethinker.

De Rudder himself was questioned and everyone who had the slightest knowledge of the case. The freethinker understood Flemish and the doctor did not, so it was the former's task to translate the testimony. As the evidence piled up, the merchant was shaken in his antireligious views. Finally, he became completely convinced that this cure could have none but a supernatural explanation, and he said so in his report.

Pierre De Rudder died of pneumonia March 22, 1898, at the age of sixty-four. This was twenty-three years after he was cured at Oostacker. Dr. van Hoestenberghe obtained permission to exhume the body and amputate the legs. This was done on May 24, 1899. Several reproductions of the leg bones have been made in plaster and copper. One of these hangs in the Medical Bureau at Lourdes, and there is another in the residence of the Jesuit Fathers at Oostacker.

An examination of the bones discloses:

1. The left leg shows traces of the double fracture. The upper part of the leg had been drawn backward during eight years by the flexor muscles of the thigh, and as a consequence the bones are not quite straight. Yet, the leg was repaired in such a way that it bore the same weight as the right leg.

2. The surface of the bones of the left leg is covered with numerous little pock marks, the result of being diseased for so long. At the point of juncture, however, there is a piece of perfectly healthy bone between the pieces that had been severed. This section is perfectly smooth and is whiter than the rest. It is more than an inch long. *This piece of bone was instantaneously created while De Rudder was at the shrine and cannot be explained on natural grounds.*

3. The two legs are exactly the same length. This is most remarkable when it is remembered that there had been a constant loss of bone material because of the nature of the

disease and that Dr. Affenear had removed a section of bone.

This question is sometimes asked: "As long as God was curing De Rudder, why did he not restore his leg to the exact condition in which it was before the accident?"

Not only in De Rudder's case, but in almost every cure which has taken place through the intercession of Our Lady of Lourdes, there remains some evidence of the previous disease. This mark in no way interferes with the effectiveness of the cure. The cure is complete; the patient is as well as he ever was, but this telltale mark remains. Why?

No one can answer this question, because no one can speak for God. Without being presumptuous, however, one can suggest a possible answer. When God works a cure of this kind, isn't it possible that He wishes its miraculous nature made manifest? In a case such as De Rudder's, if no trace had been left of the injury, many skeptics would have denied that the leg had ever been broken. With the evidence of the fracture so plain, such a denial is impossible.

Chapter XX

A DOUBLE CURE

THE Paris Express sped through the night. A thick blanket of snow covered the quiet French countryside. Inside the second last coach, four postal workers busily sorted letters. It was bitterly cold, and their fingers grew numb as they performed their task. Every so often one of the men walked over to the little stove and warmed himself and then went back to his work.

Suddenly, the four men looked at each other questioningly. The train was stopping. They had traveled this line often enough to know that the train shouldn't stop here near Angoulême. The engineer was probably having some trouble. But what a place to stop at midnight! They were on the verge of an incline and had just gone around a bend; a train coming behind them would not be able to see the rear lights. The dread thought struck them all — another express had left Bordeaux just ten minutes behind them!

Hardly had this thought come to them when they heard a dull rumbling sound. They had about two seconds to realize their danger, and then the crash came. They remembered no more.

The coach was telescoped. One of the postal clerks was killed instantly. Two others were maimed for life. Gabriel Gargam, the fourth of the postal clerks, and the subject of this chapter, was thrown 55 feet and lay unconscious in the snow all night. He was found at seven o'clock in the morning and taken to the Angoulême hospital. When he came to, he found that he was cut and bruised all over, that his collarbone was fractured, and that he was unable to move.

The fracture and the wounds healed fairly quickly, but there were grave internal disorders which would not heal. He was paralyzed from the waist down. Two weeks after the accident he was able to eat an egg, but eight months afterwards he was not able to take any nourishment at all. He was fed through a tube, but this caused such intolerable suffering that it was used only once every twenty-four hours. He also lost his power of speech.

The Orleans Railway Company was sued for damages, and Dr. Decressac, head of the Angoulême Hospital, issued a detailed report of the case. He concluded by saying that Gargam's condition "constituted a permanent infirmity, hardly susceptible of improvement, and more likely to terminate fatally."

Six months later Gargam was worse, and a supplementary report was issued. "The conclusions remain the same," wrote the doctor, "with regard to the incurability of the disease and its progressive development."

Not long after that, an infirmarian noticed that Gargam's feet were black. He rubbed one of the feet and was horrified to see the skin fall off and pus ooze out. Gangrene had set in! This was incurable. Since the patient did not suffer any pain from the gangrene, it was considered sufficient to place a covering over his feet in order to protect them from contact with the sheet.

The Orleans Railway Company tried to settle the case out of court. They could not deny that Gargam was a complete invalid, and they feared the results if the case came to trial. They offered him an annual pension of 3000 francs. The offer was rejected.

The court ordered the railway company to pay Gargam an indemnity of 60,000 francs and an annual pension of 6000 francs. The reason for this large payment was clearly stated: "The accident has made Gargam a veritable human wreck, whose intelligence alone has remained unimpaired. Struck down in the plentitude of his forces, he has seen his life ruined and his justifiable hopes of a successful career annihilated. Henceforth he will need two attendants, to give him day and night the very careful attention which is necessary if life is to be preserved."

The company's agent at Angoulême examined Gargam and advised the company to pay him 12,000 francs a year without an indemnity. The company would gain thereby, he said, because Gargam could not live very long.

The company did not follow this advice. Instead it appealed to a higher court. Again the court ruled in the injured man's favor and said that the pension should begin from the day of the accident.

Financially, Gargam was now secure, but he faced a very dismal future, and a very short one according to the predictions of the doctors.

The possibility of going to Lourdes was mentioned to Gargam several times, but he always rejected the idea. He had not been in a church for fifteen years, and he made no secret of his lack of faith. This grieved his mother, a devout Catholic, and she prayed constantly that her son would be cured spiritually even if he could not be cured physically. His aged father who had been careless in his religious duties had become very fervent after the accident, and he prayed constantly for his son.

The surgeon at the hospital wished Gargam to undergo an operation to remedy a misplaced vertebrae, but this he refused to do. The National Pilgrimage was about to start for Lourdes. His mother and family begged him to go. Finally, he consented. The doctor was still urging him to have the operation, and this seemed the best way to get away from the doctor. Without any great amount of fervor he went to Confession and received Holy Communion, as is the custom with starting pilgrims. He was able, however, to receive only a tiny particle of the Host.

The trip to Lourdes was long and painful. Gargam was carried on a stretcher which had a piece of wood fixed

The Thirteenth and Fourteenth Station groups

Pilgrims taking water from the taps

Mr. John Traynor just before leaving on his visit to Lourdes

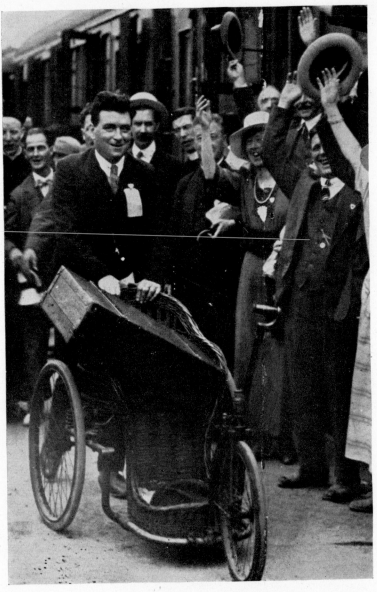

Mr. Traynor returning from Lourdes

Mr. Traynor, years after his cure, as a Brancardier at Lourdes

— Bettmann Archive

A nineteenth-century artist's conception of the grotto

vertically at one end to prevent the sheet from touching the gangrenous feet. The oesophagian tube was taken along in order to feed the patient. He was accompanied by his mother, a nurse, and a friend of the family. On the way to the train, he had a fainting fit which lasted more than a hour.

Just before reaching Lourdes, Mme. Gargam showed her son the great Crucifix which is on the hill of Calvary. "There is Lourdes, my son," she said. "Salute our Lord and ask Him to cure you."

But the patient turned his head away from the Crucifix. He still had very little faith.

It was seven o'clock in the morning of August 20, 1901, when Gabriel Gargam reached Lourdes. Twenty months had passed since the accident which had made him a helpless cripple, and Gargam was now thirty-two years old. He went first of all to the grotto where he received Communion in the same manner as he had at Angoulême. He did this because he had promised his mother that he would do so. There was no sincere devotion in his heart.

As he received the Host, he was seized with a great longing to pray. His faith suddenly returned and took complete possession of him. He loved God with his whole heart, and he laid his life at our Lady's feet. Later, he declared that this was the greatest moment of his life. No other event could compare with it, not even the one which took place later in the day.

At two o'clock in the afternoon, he was carried into the *piscines,* and he bathed in the miraculous water. He said the usual prayers fervently. He was not cured, but he found great peace.

At four o'clock, he was taken with the other patients to Rosary Square for the Blessing of the Sick. As he lay there, he seemed to take a sudden turn for the worse. He was paler than usual and more exhausted. Then he lost consciousness. The people near him touched him and found that he was cold. It was feared that he would die right there on the

Square, but the members of his party begged that he be allowed to remain for the blessing.

He regained consciousness shortly after that and heard the murmur of the praying pilgrims. With hands so thin they looked like claws, he took hold of the sides of the stretcher and tried to raise himself up. He fell back and would have tried again but a *brancardier* restrained him. The Blessed Sacrament was in front of him now. He struggled to a sitting position.

"Help me!" he cried. Two big tears rolled down his sunken cheeks. "I can walk. I feel I can!"

"Hear him, Blessed Virgin, hear him!" sobbed his mother. "He has not spoken out loud for twenty months."

A number of bystanders helped him to his feet. He stood up and took several faltering steps after the Blessed Sacrament. To the thousands witnessing the scene, it seemed that the man had risen from the dead. He was clad only in his night shirt, which resembled a shroud, and he was so thin and emaciated that he looked like a corpse. Everyone stared at him. The excitement was intense.

The people about urged him to go back and lie on the stretcher. Then he was taken to the Medical Bureau. A great throng of eager pilgrims accompanied him. Sixty doctors were present in the office and a number of newspaper correspondents. The crowd was so great and so excited that the examination had to be put off till the next day.

Back at the hospital Gargam asked for food. For months he had been unable to take any kind of nourishment without the aid of the oesophagian tube, but now he ate like anyone else. His meal consisted of soup, oysters, the wing of a chicken, and a bunch of grapes.

Visitor after visitor streamed into the hospital, and Gargam had to tell his story innumerable times. Finally, the last visitor left, and Gargam slept peacefully.

The next day, he walked unaided into the office of the Medical Bureau; he was wearing a new suit bought that morning. He was examined thoroughly. There was no more gangrene on his feet, but the healed scars could be seen. His legs were very thin. The leg muscles were missing.

"Gentlemen!" said Dr. Boissarie, the head of the Bureau, "we must first certify that from a medical point of view M. Gargam cannot walk, for he has no muscles."

Yet, when told to walk, Gargam walked across the room without difficulty.

Gargam's lawyer had been sent for, and he described the case in detail. He said the railway company had never doubted the gravity of the affliction, that every doctor consulted had declared the case incurable, and that the civil courts had described Gargam as "a veritable human wreck whose intelligence alone has remained unimpaired." All the doctors present in the Bureau, believers and nonbelievers, agreed that the case had been incurable from a medical point of view, but that it had undoubtedly been cured.

Gargam put on weight rapidly after his cure. He became strong and healthy although the vertebrae in his back remained out of place and caused a slight weakness there. For many years he came to Lourdes every summer as a *brancardier*, and no one worked harder in the service of the sick than he.

Several years later Georges Bertrim, who was at Lourdes gathering material for a book about the shrine, wished to interview Gabriel Gargam. It was very difficult to arrange such a meeting because Gargam did not wish to leave the *piscines* where he was attending the sick.

"I cannot come," he objected. "There's a miserable wretch here who comes twice a day to be bathed. He is covered with suppurating sores, and when he is undressed, he has to be cleaned like a baby in arms. I have a strong stomach, and can stand anything; if I come away, I am afraid there will be no one to take my place."

Gargam's spiritual cure was as lasting as his physical one.

Chapter XXI

"A REAL RESURRECTION"

IN SOME respects the story of John Traynor[1] is similar to that of Gabriel Gargam. Yet in many ways it is different. After their cures, the two men were *brancardiers* at Lourdes at the same time and may have discussed their cases with each other.

John Traynor was a native of Liverpool, England. His Irish mother died when he was quite young, but the faith which she instilled in her son remained with him the rest of his life. His injuries dated from World War I, when he was a soldier in the Naval Brigade of the Royal British Marines. He took part in the unsuccessful Antwerp expedition of October, 1914, and was hit in the head by shrapnel. He remained unconscious for five weeks. Later, in Egypt, he received a bullet wound in the leg. In the Dardanelles, he distinguished himself in battle but was finally brought down when he was sprayed with machine gun bullets while taking part in a bayonet charge. He was wounded in the head and chest, and one bullet went through his upper right arm and lodged under his collarbone.

As a result of these wounds, Traynor's right arm was paralyzed and the muscles atrophied. His legs were partially paralyzed, and he was epileptic. Sometimes he had as many as three fits a day. By 1916, Traynor had undergone four operations in an attempt to connect the severed muscles of this

---

[1] The facts here related are taken chiefly from the story by Father Patrick O'Connor of St. Columbans Foreign Mission Society, told in the booklet *I Met a Miracle* (St. Columbans, Nebr.), a reprint from *The Far East* Magazine.

right arm. All four operations ended in failure. By this time he had been discharged from the service. He was given a one hundred per cent pension because he was completely and permanently disabled. He spent much time in various hospitals as an epileptic patient. In April, 1920, his skull was operated on in an attempt to remove some of the shrapnel. This operation did not help his epilepsy, and it left a hole about an inch wide in his skull. The pulsating of his brain could be seen through this hole. A silver plate was inserted in order to shield the brain.

He lived on Grafton Street in Liverpool with his wife and children. He was utterly helpless. He had to be lifted from his bed to his wheelchair in the morning and back into bed at night. Arrangements had been made to have him admitted to the Mosley Hill Hospital for Incurables.

In July, 1923, Traynor heard that the Liverpool diocese was organizing a pilgrimage to Lourdes. He had always had a great devotion to the Blessed Virgin and determined to join the pilgrimage. He took a gold sovereign which he had been saving for an emergency and used it as the first payment on a ticket. At first his wife was very much disturbed by the idea of her husband making such a difficult trip. His friends tried to talk him out of it. His doctor told him the trip would be suicide. The government ministry of pensions protested against the idea. One of the priests in charge of the pilgrimage begged him to cancel his booking. All of this was to no avail. Traynor had made up his mind, and there was no changing it. When his wife saw how much he wanted to make the trip, she decided to help him. In order to raise the money for the pilgrimage, the Traynors sold some of their furniture; Mrs. Traynor pawned some of her jewelry.

There was much excitement at the railroad station the day the pilgrimage was to leave. In addition to the noise and confusion that accompanies the departure of every large pilgrimage, there was the additional hubbub caused by the curious who had come to see Traynor. His trip had aroused much interest, and at the station a great number of people crowded about his wheel chair. Newspaper reporters and photographers were on hand to cover the event. As a result of all this, Traynor reached the station platform too late to get on the first train. The second train was crowded, and once more an attempt was made to talk him out of taking the trip. Traynor, however, said that he was determined to go if he had to ride in the coal tender.

The trip was extremely trying, and Traynor was very sick. Three times, during the journey across France, the directors of the pilgrimage wished to take him off the train and put him in a hospital. Each time there was no hospital where they stopped, and so they had to keep him on board. He was more dead than alive when he reached Lourdes on July 22 and was taken to the Asile. Two Protestant girls from Liverpool, who were serving as volunteer nurses in the Asile, recognized Traynor and offered to take care of him. He gladly accepted the offer. He had several hemorrhages during his six days there and a number of epileptic fits. So bad was his condition that one woman took it upon herself to write to his wife and tell her that there was no hope for him and that he would be buried in Lourdes.

Traynor managed to bathe in the water from the grotto nine times, and he attended all the ceremonies to which the sick are taken. It was only by sheer force of will that he was able to do this. Not only were his own infirmities a serious obstacle but the *brancardiers* and others in attendance were reluctant to take him out for fear he would die on the way. Once he had an epileptic fit as he was going to the *piscines*. When he recovered, the *brancardiers* turned his chair to take him back to the Asile. He protested, but they insisted. They were forced to give in when he seized the wheel with his good hand and would not let the chair budge until it went in the direction of the baths.

On the afternoon of July 25 when he was in the bath, his paralyzed legs became suddenly agitated. He tried to get to his feet, but the *brancardiers* prevented him. They dressed him, put him back in his wheel chair, and hurried him to Rosary Square for the Blessing of the Sick. Most of the other sick were already lined up. He was the third last on the outside as one faces the church.

Let us hear in Traynor's own words what happened after that. This is the story as he told it to Father Patrick O'Connor.

"The procession came winding its way back, as usual, to the church and at the end walked the Archbishop of Rheims, carrying the Blessed Sacrament. He blessed the two ahead of me, came to me, made the Sign of the Cross with the monstrance and moved on to the next. He had just passed by, when I realized that a great change had taken place in me. My right arm, which had been dead since 1915, was violently agitated. I burst its bandages and blessed myself — for the first time in years.

"I had no sudden pain that I can recall and certainly had no vision. I simply realized that something momentous had happened. I attempted to rise from my stretcher, but the *brancardiers* were watching me. I suppose I had a bad name for my obstinacy. They held me down, and a doctor or a nurse gave me a hypo. Apparently they thought that I was hysterical and about to create a scene. Immediately after the final Benediction, they rushed me back to the Asile. I told them that I could walk and proved it by taking seven steps. I was very tired and in pain. They put me back in bed and gave me another hypo after a while.

"They had me in a small ward on the ground floor. As I was such a troublesome case, they stationed *brancardiers* in relays to watch me and keep me from doing anything foolish. Late that night, they placed a *brancardier* on guard outside the door of the ward. There were two other sick men in the room, including one who was blind.

"The effect of the hypos began to wear off during the night, but I had no full realization that I was cured. I was awake for most of the night. No lights were on.

"The chimes of the big Basilica rang the hours and half-hours as usual through the night, playing the air of the Lourdes *Ave Maria.* Early in the morning, I heard them ringing, and it seemed to me that I fell asleep at the beginning of the *Ave.* It could have been a matter of only a few seconds, but at the last stroke I opened my eyes and jumped out of bed. First, I knelt on the floor to finish the rosary I had been saying. Then I dashed for the door, pushed aside the two *brancardiers* and ran out into the passage and the open air. Previously, I had been watching the *brancardiers* and planning to evade them. I may say here that I had not walked since 1915, and my weight was down to 112 pounds.

"Dr. Marley was outside the door. When he saw the man over whom he had been watching during the pilgrimage, and whose death he had expected, push two *brancardiers* aside and run out of the ward, he fell back in amazement. Out in the open now, I ran toward the Grotto, which is about two or three hundred yards from the Asile. This stretch of ground was graveled then, not paved, and I was barefoot. I ran the whole way to the grotto without getting the least mark or cut on my bare feet. The *brancardiers* were running after me, but they could not catch up with me. When they reached the grotto, there I was on my knees, still in my night clothes, praying to our Lady and thanking her. All I knew was that I should thank her and the grotto was the place to do it. The *brancardiers* stood back, afraid to touch me."

A strange feature of Traynor's case was that he did not completely realize what had happened to him. He knew that a great favor had been bestowed upon him and that he should be thankful, but he had no idea of the magnitude of the favor. He was completely dazed. It did not seem strange to him that he was walking, and he could not figure out why everyone was staring at him. He did not remember how gravely ill he had been for many years.

A crowd of people gathered about Traynor while he was praying at the grotto. After about twenty minutes, he arose from his knees, surprised and rather annoyed by the audience he had attracted. The people fell back to allow him to pass. At the crowned statute of our Lady, he stopped and knelt again. His mother had taught him that he should always make some sacrifice when he wished to venerate the Virgin. He had no money to give. The few shillings he had left after buying a railroad ticket, he had spent to buy rosaries and medals for his wife and children. He therefore made the only sacrifice he could think of: he promised our Lady that he would give up cigarettes.

The news of his cure had spread rapidly, and a great crowd was waiting at the Asile. Traynor could not understand what they were doing there. He went in and got dressed. Then he went into the washroom. A number of men were there ahead of him.

"Good morning, gentlemen!" said Traynor cheerily.

But there was no answer. The men just looked at him; they were too overcome to speak.

Traynor was puzzled. Why was everyone acting so strangely this morning?

When he got back to his ward, a priest who was visiting at Lourdes came in and said, "Is there anyone who can serve Mass?"

"Yes, I can," Traynor volunteered.

The priest who knew nothing yet about the cure accepted the offer, and Traynor served Mass in the chapel of the Asile. It did not seem a bit out of the ordinary to be doing so.

In the dining room of the Asile where Traynor went to eat his breakfast, the other patients stared at him in amazement. Later when he strolled outdoors, the crowd that had gathered there made a rush at him. Surprised and disconcerted he made a quick retreat into the enclosure.

A Mr. Cunningham, who was also on the pilgrimage, came to talk to him. The visitor spoke casually, but it was evident that he was making a great effort to control his excitement.

"Good morning, Jack. Are you feeling all right?"

"Yes, Mr. Cunningham, quite all right. Are you feeling all right?" Then he came to the matter that was puzzling him. "What are all those people doing outside?"

"They're there, Jack, because they are glad to see you."

"Well, it's nice of them, and I'm glad to see them, but I wish they'd leave me alone."

Mr. Cunningham told him that one of the priests of the pilgrimage — the one who had opposed his coming — wished to see him. There was much difficulty getting through the crowd, but they finally got to the hotel where the priest was waiting. The priest asked him if he was all right. All this solicitude was most bewildering.

"Yes, I'm quite well," Traynor answered, "and I hope you feel well, too."

The priest broke down and began to cry.

Traynor traveled home in a first-class compartment despite all his protests. As they were going across France, Archbishop Keating of Liverpool came into his compartment. Traynor knelt to receive his blessing. The Archbishop bade him rise.

"John, I think I should be getting your blessing," he said.

Traynor did not know what the Archbishop meant.

The Archbishop led him over to the bed, and they both sat down. Looking at Traynor closely, His Excellency said, "John, do you realize how ill you have been and that you have been miraculously cured by the Blessed Virgin?"

"Suddenly," Traynor later told Father O'Connor, "everything came back to me, the memory of my years of illness and the sufferings of the journey to Lourdes and how ill I had been in Lourdes itself. I began to cry, and the Archbishop began to cry, and we both sat there, crying like two children. After a little talk with him, I felt composed. Now I realized fully what had happened."

Someone suggested to Traynor that he telegraph his wife. Instead of telling her that he had been completely cured, he merely said, "Am better — Jack." His wife was very much pleased to receive this message. She had been very much upset when the woman in the pilgrimage had told her that he was dying. But she was not prepared for the glorious news that was to come! She was the only one who was not, for the story had been in the Liverpool papers. Since she had not happened to see the story, those about her decided not to tell her. They thought it would be nicer to surprise her.

It seemed that all Liverpool was at the station to greet the cured man upon his return. When Mrs. Traynor reached the platform, she told who she was and asked to be allowed through the crowd.

"Well," said the official in charge, "all I can say is that Mr. Traynor must be a Mohammedan, because there are seventy or eighty Mrs. Traynors on the platform now."

In an attempt to save Traynor from being crushed by the crowd which was growing every minute, the railway company stopped the train before it got to the station. The Archbishop walked toward the crowd. He asked the people to restrain their enthusiasm when they saw Traynor and to disperse peacefully after they had had a look at him. They promised that they would do so.

Despite this promise there was a stampede when Traynor appeared on the platform. The police had to clear a passage for him to pass through.

The joy of Traynor's family upon his return and their deep gratitude to Our Lady of Lourdes could never be put into words. The cured man went into the coal and hauling business and had no trouble lifting 200-pound sacks of coal. He went back to Lourdes every summer to act as a *brancardier*. He died on the eve of the Feast of the Immaculate Conception in 1943. The cause of his death was in no way related to the wounds which had been cured at Lourdes.

The two non-Catholic girls who looked after Traynor at Lourdes came into the Church as a result of the cure. Their family followed their example, and so did the Anglican minister of the church they had been attending. A great number of conversions in Liverpool resulted from the miracle.

Although the cure took place in 1923, the Medical Bureau waited till 1926 to issue its report. Traynor was examined again, and it was found that his cure was permanent. "His right arm which was like a skeleton has recovered all its muscles. The hole near his temple has completely disappeared. He had a certificate from Dr. McConnell of Liverpool attesting that he had not had an epileptic attack since 1923. . . .

"It is known that when the important nerves have been severed, if their regeneration has not been effected (after the most successful operations this would take at least a year) they contract rapidly and become dried up as it were, and certain parts mortify and disappear. In Mr. Traynor's case, for the cure of his paralyzed arm, new parts had to be created and seamed together. All these things were done simultaneously and instantaneously. At the same time occurred the instant repair of the brain injuries as is proved by the sudden and definite disappearance of the paralysis of both legs and of the epileptic attacks. Finally, a third work was effected which closed the orifice in the brain box. It is a real resurrection which the beneficiary attributes to the power of God and the merciful intercession of Our Lady of Lourdes. The mode of production of this prodigious cure is absolutely outside and beyond the forces of nature."

As is usual in such cures, John Traynor retained souvenirs of his former afflictions. The right hand did not hang quite normally, and the right forearm was a little less thick than the left. A slight depression was the only trace that was left of the hole in the skull.

If John Traynor and Gabriel Gargam ever discussed their cases and compared notes while both were serving as *brancardiers*, they must have been amused by one point. Gargam succeeded in having his pension from the railway company discontinued. The British War Pension Ministry, however, insisted upon paying Traynor's pension till the end of his life. They had examined him thoroughly and found him incurable. They did not care what the Lourdes Medical

Bureau said or what any of the doctors who examined Traynor after his return from Lourdes reported. It did not matter that he was engaged in the most strenuous kind of work. They had pronounced him incurable, and incurable he was. This decision was never revoked.

CHAPTER XXII

THE UNCURED

OF THE 10,000 sick and afflicted who make the pilgrimage to Lourdes every year, only a small per cent are favored by a cure. The others leave the shrine in the same physical condition in which they arrived. Many of these unfortunate people have traveled great distances, and their trips have caused them immense discomfort and, in some cases, intense physical pain. Frequently, they have made a considerable financial sacrifice in order to visit the shrine.

In the case of a Gargam or a Traynor these sacrifices have been definitely worth while and come under the head of sound investments. But what about the persons who leave Lourdes uncured? Do they feel that the trip has been made in vain? Are they bitter and disillusioned? Do they feel that the Blessed Virgin has neglected them?

These questions occurred to J. B. McAllister, an American writer, a few years ago, as he saw the rows and rows of sick people in front of the grotto. He resolved to inquire about the uncured. At the desk of the Hospitalité, he found a man who spoke English. To this man he put the questions that had been troubling him. Some time later, Mr. McAllister related the interview.[1]

"True," said the man, "only a few are cured, but many are helped. Of the uncured, none despair. I often interview patients before they leave. I have never seen a case, even

---

[1] In Commonweal.

the worst, downcast. They go away filled with hope. They do not say 'adieu' but 'au revoir.'"

Mr. McAllister expressed his astonishment at the statement that none despair. Such a thing seemed incredible. The man repeated the words.

"None despair! I will give you an example. A lady had come to Lourdes several summers without being cured. Last summer during Benediction, the lady beside her was cured. That evening, a friend complained that she should have been the favored one since she came oftener. 'No,' she said, 'the lady beside me was worse than I. It was quite natural that she should be cured and not I!' The words you usually hear are, 'God's will be done.'"

As they were talking, McAllister noticed that the man was wearing armpads and that two crutches leaned against the wall behind him. What was this man's story, McAllister wondered. What was he doing here, serving without pay during the hottest part of the summer? He ventured to ask the man about himself. The clerk replied that there was not time to tell the story now, but that we would relate it in a letter.

Some months later, the letter arrived. M. H. Lemarchand, for this was the man's name, a native of Brest, had been crippled from birth. He longed to go to Lourdes where he hoped he might be cured, but he and his sister were orphans and could not afford to make the trip. The years flew by. World War I came along, and the pilgrimage was out of the question. Finally in 1920, he and his sister were able to go to Lourdes. The longing of a lifetime was fulfilled.

"The first thing we did on arriving," said M. Lemarchand in his letter, "was to go to the grotto. My first impression was very deep and made up of hope and sadness. Sadness at the sight of the sufferers we passed; sadness at having kept away so long. Of hope for my cure. During twenty-four years, I had thought of Lourdes and of going there — and I was here. My first station at the grotto was a weeping one. Why did

I weep? I cannot tell, but such was my first prayer. The Blessing of the Sick was another occasion of shedding tears, but this time they were tears of pity."

Two days later it was time to leave. The farewell was heart-rending, "not that I was disappointed, but it seemed I was leaving my home and best friends; so I promised to come the next year."

And come the next year he did, for eight days this time.

"I still prayed for my cure. But on the second day at Lourdes, while I was sitting among the sick during Benediction, I began to be ashamed of myself. On my right, a blind woman sat rigid in her chair; on my left lay a consumptive. I looked around at all those sufferers, and then up to the green mountains and higher to the sky. I could see and I could move about, having the free use of my ears and tongue and arms. I had not known sickness or disease — and I was praying for my cure! I started praying for the blind woman and the consumptive. Since that moment, I have felt that I ought to think of others and not myself."

The following year, he and his sister came back again. The year after that his sister, a nurse, worked in the baths. He felt useless until it occurred to him to offer himself for clerical work. His knowledge of French and English proved very valuable, and his services were readily accepted. He felt like a new man; he was doing something to help the sick. He continued to go back every summer during his vacation.

"Perhaps it sounds foolish," he said, "to speak of the happiness I have found at Lourdes, I who went to Lourdes to be cured and am still a cripple. But I have found contentment, and my soul has been cured. And for more persons than anyone knows, Lourdes has done the same thing."

This same story is told by virtually all the uncured. At Lourdes they gain a new peace. They become resigned to their afflictions and see them as crosses which God has asked them to bear.

The most famous case of an American uncured is that of

Frederick Snite, "the man in the iron lung." Snite had contracted infantile paralysis while traveling in China in 1936 and had been lying flat on his back in a respirator or "iron lung" almost constantly since that time. He was unable to breathe if he was out of it for more than a few moments at a time. His case had aroused the sympathy of the American people.

Naturally, there was great interest in 1939 when it was learned that Snite intended to take a trip to Lourdes. The journey entailed much preparation. A trailer had to be taken along so the iron lung could be transported over the roads of France, and a retinue of nurses had to accompany the young man. When the party left New York, newspaper and newsreel photographers took many pictures. The trailer had to be taken on board ship by means of derricks.

What a time this would have been for a miracle! After all the publicity the trip had received, suppose Snite should come back no longer "the man in the iron lung." Suppose he should walk down the gangplank just like any other passenger. The sensation caused by John Traynor's return to Liverpool would be as nothing compared with this. The ships going to Europe would not be able to hold all the people who would wish to visit Lourdes.

But nothing of the kind happened. When Frederick Snite returned to the United States, he was still in his iron lung. Many people smiled knowingly as if to say, "Well, what did he expect?" There was a general feeling that Snite must be terribly disappointed and on the verge of despair. The trip had been entirely in vain.

In vain? Frederick Snite did not think so. He had not gone to Lourdes seeking a miracle. He had said that if our Lady saw fit to help him he would be very pleased, but he was going primarily to pay her homage.

"Life here at Lourdes is so wonderful," he wrote in his diary, "such a series of unending thrills that I find it difficult to record my reactions. Everyone is happy, happy because they are in a place apart from the world — a place seemingly halfway to heaven. Here there is no talk of war, of politics, of business; life here is a prayer. Is it any wonder we are happy?"

After attending the procession of the Blessed Sacrament, he wrote, "Seeing some of the other sick people makes me feel very fortunate."

His doctors begged him not to bathe in the *piscines.* Leaving the iron lung and going into the cold water would be suicide, they said. But Snite was deaf to their entreaties. In his diary he wrote, "Early this afternoon I had another new experience — a bath in the famous Lourdes water. . . . In that I had to leave the respirator during the bath, I was quite nervous and excited. Everything went smoothly, however, and I was soon glad that I had decided to do it. The water was very cold, but I did not mind it. There was some kind of happiness in connection with it which I am unable to analyze, therefore unable to record. All I can say is that I was glad for the opportunity."

He has told friends that while bathing, a wonderful feeling of peace came over him, a feeling he had never before experienced.

A few days later, he had his second bath. This time he was only slightly excited. Everything went as smoothly as before, and the water hardly seemed cold.

On Friday, June 2, Snite wrote in his diary, "And so tomorrow is Saturday — the ninth day of our stay and Sunday the last day. I have not in any way given up or lost hope. I am praying very, very fervently, and if nothing happens, as I have so often said before, God certainly knows what is best for Him, for me, and for the world in general."

The entry for June 4 concludes with these two short sentences: "Our pilgrimage is at an end. God's will be done."

If you were to ask Frederick Snite or any of those close to him whether the trip was made in vain, the answer would be an emphatic "No." The feeling which the trip left with him is shown by the fact that he has named one of his daughters Bernadette. Everyone marvels that Snite can be so cheerful despite his affliction. Those who should know say that this is due in no small part to the strength given him by Our Lady of Lourdes.

"Of the uncured, none despair." All go away filled with hope, with a new feeling of strength. The trip to Lourdes is never made in vain.

Chapter XXIII

THE WOMAN SHALL CONQUER

T
HE trip to Lourdes is never made in vain, and no one ever has recourse to Our Lady of Lourdes in vain.

In the story of Lourdes one fact stands out like a great beacon of hope in the darkness that surrounds us. That fact is that our Lady *wants* to help us and that she is making every effort to do so. She did not have to leave her heavenly home to appear to Bernadette. She was under no obligation to tell the world that it should do penance. Had the people listened to the teachings of our Lord, they would have known this. It was not necessary for her to ask that a shrine be built at Lourdes, and it is most certainly not necessary for her to go on working miracles there year after year.

She did these things because she is a kind and loving mother who saw her children straying from the path that had been laid out for them and becoming lost in a morass of indifferentism. She wished to extend them a helping hand before they were lost forever.

Today, the world faces new problems, and religion is again under attack from many quarters. Our personal trials and afflictions are so burdensome that sometimes we think we can hardly go on. It will always be so. Satan never rests in his determination to block the road to heaven. As soon as one obstacle is removed he raises several new ones in its place.

But through all our trials we can take comfort in the fact that Our Lady of Lourdes is still ready to help us. Was it by chance that Franz Werfel happened upon Lourdes and went forth to sing the Song of Bernadette during history's greatest war? Those who have studied the ways of our Lady are inclined to say no. Werfel himself, at a testimonial dinner given in his honor, said: "I am not the one to be congratulated; I am not the real author of this story; I am but an instrument acting for someone else; the real author is the Blessed Virgin Mary."

During the war and during the years of readjustment to follow, mankind will be sorely tried. We shall be more than ever in need of our Lady's help, and she seems to be making every effort to extend that aid. It is encouraging to reflect that in these turbulent times Our Lady of Lourdes is better known than she has ever been before, especially on this side of the Atlantic, and that devotion to her has increased greatly.

Our Lady of Lourdes is begging us to come to her. If we do so, humbly and sincerely, she will not fail us.

THE LITERATURE OF LOURDES

IT IS customary to have a bibliography at the end of a book of this kind. In the case of Lourdes, however, something more than a mere listing of titles, authors, and publishers seems to be called for. The author considers the works he has consulted as part of the story of the shrine itself, and as such believes they deserve a chapter to themselves.

Henri Lasserre is often called the Historian of Lourdes, because it was he who wrote the first comprehensive report of the apparitions. In 1862, Lasserre, a brilliant lawyer and journalist, lost his eyesight. At the urging of a Protestant friend, he wrote to Abbe Peyramale for some Lourdes water. As soon as the water was applied to his eyes, his sight returned. In gratitude, he set out to write the story of the apparitions which had taken place just four years before. He interviewed Bernadette, Abbe Peyramale, and hundreds of other persons who could give him firsthand information. He traveled to all parts of France gathering his material.

Our Lady of Lourdes was published in 1869, while Bernadette was still alive. It became a phenomenal success at once. It has been translated into more than eighty dialects and languages and has gone through several hundred editions. It was signally honored by a brief from Pope Pius IX.

More recent works are more accurate than Lasserre's, because new evidence has come to light since his time. In places he seems to have supplied more details than the evidence warranted. His book is worth reading, however, because it contains so much of the first devotional flavor and because Lasserre has such a pleasing style. An inexpensive abridged translation has been published recently by the Catechetical Guild of St. Paul, Minnesota.

Miraculous Episodes of Our Lady of Lourdes by Lasserre was published fourteen years after his first book about the shrine. In it he recounts in detail some of the miracles worked through the intercession of Our Lady of Lourdes. One of these cures is his own. An English translation was published in 1884 by Burns and Oates, London.

The Appearances of the Blessed Virgin Mary at the Grotto of Lourdes — Personal Souvenirs of an Eyewitness was written by J. B. Estrade who has been quoted a number of times in the course of this work. Estrade's book has been criticized on the grounds that it is not entirely accurate, that he used his imagination to supply details that had slipped his mind. This is quite possible. The book was not written until twenty years after the events described, and he confessed that it was very difficult to remember all the details after so long a time.

Even though Estrade's book may not be entirely accurate it is worth reading as the account of an eye witness. He was the only other person present, for example, when Jacomet interviewed Bernadette. His story is that of a scoffer who became converted when he could not deny the evidence. He was one of the "intellectuals" of Lourdes and so was in an excellent position to tell how the story of the apparitions was received in those circles. An English translation was published in 1912 by the Art and Book Company, Ltd., of Westminster, England.

Pere Cros, S.J., did more than anyone else to gather all available testimony regarding Bernadette and the apparitions. His book *N. D. de Lourdes, Recits et Mystères* was published in 1901 by Beauchesne, Paris, and his great three volume *Histoire de Notre Dame de Lourdes d'pres le Documents et les Temoins* was published in 1925 by the same company. Pere Cros interviewed every witness who might be able to throw light on even the smallest of details and examined all pertinent documents in civil and ecclesiastical archives. All recent biographers have leaned heavily upon Pere Cros. This explains the fact that, generally speaking, the biographies of Bernadette which were written after 1901 are more accurate than those written before that date, and the ones written since 1925 are the most accurate of all. It is to be hoped that Pere Cros's works will be translated into English in the not-to-distant future.

La Confidente de L'Immaculée was issued in 1912 by the Sisters of Charity and Christian Instruction of Nevers, the order to which Bernadette belonged. In 1915 an English translation entitled *Bernadette of Lourdes* was published by the Bureau of the Immaculate Conception, New York. This book, as might be expected, is extremely valuable as a record of Bernadette's years in the convent at Nevers.

Bernadette, Child of Mary by L. L. McReavy (B. Herder Book Co., St. Louis, 1933) is interesting and authoritative.

Bernadette of Lourdes is the title of a booklet by Rev. C. C. Martindale, S.J., and published by the Catholic Truth Society of London. It is very accurate.

Bernadette of Lourdes is also the title of a booklet by Father Ralph, S.V.D., published in 1939 by the Mission Press of Techny, Ill.

Bernadette of Lourdes by Margaret Gray Blanton (Longmans, Green and Company, New York, 1939) can be recommended wholeheartedly. Mrs. Blanton, a Protestant, spared no effort to make sure that her facts were accurate. Such exhaustive records are available, she tells us, that it was necessary to guess at nothing. "If the night were clear and cold or the stones sharp, it has been so testified. If she thought, or he wished, or they believed, it has been so testified."

A person whose interest in Bernadette has been aroused by *The Song of Bernadette* (The Viking Press, New York, 1942) and who would like to know the exact facts would do well to read Mrs. Blanton's book or one of the other recent books named above. Werfel's book, it must be remembered, is fiction, and many facts have been altered to make them conform to the pattern of the novel.

What facts in *The Song of Bernadette* are not quite accurate? It is not possible to list them all, but a few might be mentioned.

The book implies that Antoine Nicolau, the miller, was in love with Bernadette. The movie made even more of a point of this. The truth is that Antoine was in awe of Bernadette and felt that she was a saint, but he was not in love with her. At the time of the apparitions he was at least twenty-eight years old; she was fourteen and looked twelve.

Mother M. Vauzous, the mistress of novices at Nevers, did not teach Bernadette at Lourdes. Mother Vauzous was very strict with Bernadette because she was of the mistaken opinion that the girl needed humbling. There is no reason to suppose that she was full of doubt, suspicion, pride, and envy.

The Lady did not show Bernadette the spring after Abbe Peyramale had asked her to make the rose bush bloom, as if she were answering his request for a miracle. The spring was discovered on February 25; the priest asked for the blooming rose bush on March 2.

Those are probably the biggest departures from fact. There are many smaller ones. Bernadette's father was not a heavy drinker. The grotto of Massabielle was not a city dump. Louis Bourriette, the stone cutter who was cured of his blindness, was not illiterate. Abbe Peyramale could not have gone to Bernadette when she was dying, for he had died seventeen months before. There is no certainty that the Blessed Virgin appeared to Bernadette when she was dying.

On a few points the motion picture has strayed farther from the true story than the book has. The movie, for example, gives the impression that Bernadette was "railroaded" to the convent. This was most certainly not the case. She wished to become a Carmelite but could not be admitted to that order because of her poor health. In the movie the Imperial Prosecutor, Dutour, is an atheist who is finally converted when he is dying of a throat ailment. In reality, he was a fairly religious man who simply did not believe Bernadette's story and could not believe it despite all the evidence. In later years he admitted that he had made a mistake. There was no dramatic conversion, and he had no throat ailment.

The list could be extended further, but this is enough to show that one who wishes the complete, accurate account of what happened at Lourdes should go farther than *The Song of Bernadette.* This is no reflection upon either the book or the movie as works of art. Werfel freely admits that he altered certain facts to suit his purpose although his story is essentially true.

So much for the books which deal only with Bernadette and the apparitions. Now for a quick glance at those which are about the shrine itself and the miracles which have taken place there.

Les Foules de Lourdes by J. K. Huysmans stands out among the books about the shrine. An English translation, *The Crowds of Lourdes* was published in 1925 by Burns, Oates and Washbourne of London.

The beginning of Huysmans' literary career was similar to Zola's. In fact, Huysmans was a disciple of Zola. His first books belonged to the realistic school and depicted all that was base and vile in man. In 1895 he passed a week at the Trappist monastery at Issigny and was deeply impressed by the monastic life. Soon afterward he became a Catholic and spent the last twelve years of his life fighting for his faith. *Les Foules* was his last book, and it was written in answer to Zola's novel.

Huysmans remained the realist after his conversion. Certain passages of *Les Foules,* such as his account of his visit to the hospital, should not be read by anyone with a weak stomach. He was also a keen observer and saw things which most people would miss. To him, the candles burning in the grotto are more than just candles. His description of them is quoted in Chapter XIV of this book.

Brilliant though he was, Huysmans had his limitations. He was less than just to Abbe Peyramale, whom he accused of tearing down the old parish church, full of memories of Bernadette, in order to make room for a "clumsy monument trying to beat the Basilica with its frightful colored windows and its false glitter." The truth is that the new church was begun long before the old was demolished. The old one was torn down not to make room for the new but because it has been irreparably damaged by fire. Huysmans complained constantly of the ugliness of Lourdes and said, quite seriously, that the ugliness was inspired by Satan. Yet, most visitors find Lourdes anything but ugly. All such defects are minor and do not detract from the excellence of the work. Huysmans would not have been Huysmans if he had written in any other way.

Lourdes, Its Inhabitants, Its Pilgrims, and Its Miracles by Richard F. Clarke, S.J. (Benziger Brothers, New York, 1888), is one of the few earlier books about Lourdes which is still in print. Its title describes its contents. It is a good description of the Lourdes of its day which to a large extent is still very much the same today. The last two chapters treat of Bernadette and the apparitions.

Lourdes, A History of Its Apparitions and Cures by Georges Bertrim translated by Mrs. Philip Gibbs (Benziger Brothers, New York, 1908) is valuable for its detailed description of how cures are investigated and for its accounts of certain cures. The first three chapters are devoted to Bernadette and the apparitions. M. Bertrim is also the author of the article about Lourdes in *The Catholic Encyclopedia*.

The Glories of Lourdes by the Chanoine Justin Rousseil, translated by Rev. Joseph Murphy, S.J. (Burns, Oates and Washbourne, London, 1922) contains information not found in most books: the early history of the district in which Lourdes is located; a consideration as to why the Blessed Virgin appeared to Bernadette; accounts of the persons connected with the story of Lourdes, such as Abbe Peyramale,

Monseigneur Laurence, Dr. Boissarie, etc.; and explanation of the liturgy of Lourdes.

Heaven's Recent Wonders by Dr. Boissarie, translated by Rev. C. Van Der Donckt (Frederick Pustet and Company, New York, 1909) is one of a number of books written by the man who was for many years head of the Medical Bureau. Dr. Boissarie's accounts of the cures are, of course, most authentic.

The Secret of Lourdes by Stuart Martin (Frank-Maurice, New York, 1924) is principally a description of the Lourdes of 1923. Three of the twelve chapters are devoted to Bernadette, the apparitions, and the final investigation. The work of the Medical Bureau is described and accounts of several cures are given.

The Wonder of Lourdes by John Oxenham (Longmans, Green and Company, New York, 1924) is a Protestant's view of Lourdes. Few books have been written in a spirit of greater reverence. Unfortunately, it is now out of print.

Up and Down Lourdes by Edith Cowell (Benziger Brothers, New York, 1923) is a personal account of a visit to the shrine. After arriving in Lourdes, Miss Cowell volunteered to serve in the refectory of the Asile. In this little book she gives an account of her experiences and also her impressions of the shrine.

Lourdes by Aileen Mary Clegg (B. Herder Book Co., St. Louis, 1929) is a very readable description of the shrine and the ceremonies that take place there. The chapters dealing with the Mass of the Sick, the *piscines,* and the Blessing of the Sick are particularly good.

Tramping to Lourdes by John Gibbons (P. J. Kenedy and Sons, New York, 1927) describes a pilgrimage which Mr. Gibbons made to Lourdes in order to beg our Lady's intercession for his baby son who was very ill. After crossing the English Channel he walked every step of the way to Lourdes. Of the 213 pages in the book, 176 are devoted to the 600 mile walk, so the reader who is expecting a book about Lourdes will be disappointed. The last 37 pages, in which the author describes his work as a *brancardier,* are very interesting. Later, Mr. Gibbons wrote another book *What Is This Lourdes?* (Methuen and Co., London, 1936) in which he told more about the shrine.

Lourdes in the High Pyrenees by Cecilia Mary Young (Buechler Publishing Company, Belleville, Ill., 1932) is divided into three parts. The first part is devoted to the apparitions. The second part is a vivid description of modern Lourdes: the town, the park, the grotto, the spring, the baths, the Medical Bureau. The third part, "Lourdes and the Blessed Sacrament" is also very good.

At the Shrine of God's Friends by Frederick M. Lynk, S.V.D. (The Mission Press, Techny, Ill., 1933) is an account of Father Lynk's visits to twenty-seven shrines, the last of which is Lourdes.

A Modern Miracle — The Case of Peter de Rudder by Rev. Felix Rankin, S.J. (Catholic Truth Society, London, 1905) is a booklet giving a full account of De Rudder's remarkable cure. The case is also described in several other of the books listed here.

I Met A Miracle by Rev. Patrick O'Connor (The Far East, St. Columbans, Nebraska, 1944) is a booklet describing the cure of John Traynor. It is based upon a personal interview with Traynor. Photographs add to the interest of the absorbing story. This is a reprint of an article which appeared originally in the magazine, *The Far East.*

A number of very good magazine articles have also been written about Lourdes. Some of them are listed below by magazine and date. The titles of the articles are omitted in order to save space.

The Catholic World, June, 1895; July, 1909; May, 1924; September, 1924; April, 1925; September, 1925; October, 1925; September, 1926; August, 1927; February, 1928; February, 1930; February, 1940.

The Commonweal, November 6, 1929; May 6, 1931; August 18, 1933; February 23, 1934; March 30, 1934; May 3, 1935; December 15, 1939; May 29, 1942.

Catholic Digest, August, 1937; June, 1939; September, 1939; April, 1942; August, 1943; September, 1943; January, 1944.

Columbia, June, 1944.

Fortune, January, 1934.
This article *The Miracles of Lourdes* deserves special mention because it is a creditable and comprehensive report on Lourdes by a secular magazine. Such articles are very rare. Of the thousands of articles listed in the *Reader's Guide to Periodical Literature* for the twenty-one year period between 1924 and 1925 only three are about Lourdes. One of these is in a magazine which has since suspended publication and which is very difficult to secure. The second is short and superficial in treatment. The third speaks of the wonderful psychic healings at Lourdes and misses the point altogether, for there is no mention of the supernatural. (The article in *Fortune* is not among these three, for *Fortune* is not indexed in the *Reader's Guide*.) Lourdes, with its great number of amazing cures, should be one of the greatest journalistic stories of our times, but the magazines are afraid to touch it.

This list of books, booklets, and magazine articles is, of course, not complete. It consists merely of the works which have come to the attention of the author in the preparation of this volume. There are, no doubt, many other valuable works, but this list, incomplete as it is, may be of some assistance to anyone who wishes to do more reading on the fascinating subject of Lourdes.